NEW YORK CITY MUSEUM GUIDE

EDITED BY

Candace Ward

DOVER PUBLICATIONS, INC.

NEW YORK

Copyright

Copyright © 1995 by Dover Publications, Inc.
All rights reserved under Pan American and International Copyright Conventions.

Published in Canada by General Publishing Company, Ltd., 30 Lesmill Road, Don Mills,
Toronto, Ontario.
Published in the United Kingdom by Constable and Company, Ltd., 3 The Lanchesters,
162–164 Fulham Palace Road, London W6 9ER.

Bibliographical Note

New York City Museum Guide is a new work, first published by Dover Publications, Inc.,
in 1995.

Library of Congress Cataloging-in-Publication Data

New York City museum guide / edited by Candace Ward.
    p.   cm.
  Includes index.
  ISBN 0-486-28639-8
  1. Museums—New York (N.Y.)—Guidebooks. 2. New York (N.Y.)—Guidebooks.
I. Ward, Candace.
AM13.N5N48 1995
069'.09747'1—dc20   95-14775
                                                                  CIP

Manufactured in the United States of America
Dover Publications, Inc., 31 East 2nd Street, Mineola, N.Y. 11501

CONTENTS

Contents

INTRODUCTION

The five boroughs of New York City—the Bronx, Brooklyn, Manhattan, Queens and Staten Island—encompass a world of cultural offerings, from traditional museums to environmental centers to historical landmarks. The *Guide to New York City Museums* provides a practical reference source to over 130 of these institutions. Many of those included are well known—the Statue of Liberty, the American Museum of Natural History and the Metropolitan Museum of Art, for example. Others are less familiar—the New York City Fire Museum, Socrates Sculpture Park, the Maritime Industry Museum at Fort Schuyler, the Chassidic Art Institute and the Staten Island Ferry Collection—but each will hold pleasant surprises for even the most seasoned museumgoers.

The entries are arranged alphabetically (within each borough) and borough maps are provided on which museum locations are identified by entry numbers. The most accessible bus routes and subway stations for each site are listed as well. Visitors unfamiliar with the city's public transportation system (operated by the New York City Transit Authority) will find traveling by bus and subway convenient and safe. If you plan to travel by subway, familiarizing yourself with a subway map (free subway and bus maps are available at all token booths) can make travel easier, but if reading maps is not your strong suit, transit personnel will provide directions on request. Traveling by bus allows you to observe the city, providing an inexpensive tour. At many bus stops riders will find "Guide-A-Ride" signs with a map and the route(s) for that stop. Once aboard, do not hesitate to ask the driver to announce your stop if you are unsure where to get off. The NYCTA also operates a phone service (718-330-1234) with operators who provide bus and subway directions, fare and other service information.

Designed for educators and students as well as tourists, this volume also provides information about how to arrange group and school tours. Some of the institutions provide research facilities or access to their collections for scholars and researchers, and many offer educational classes, seminars, lectures, symposia and film or video series. Readers interested in taking advantage of these offerings are urged to call individual facilities for more details.

Every effort was made to provide the most accurate and current information available. In any guidebook, however, information can become dated. For this reason, descriptions of each institution focus on permanent collections and exhibits, and phone numbers are provided for visitors to call and receive up-to-date information on current offerings and special or seasonal events.

MANHATTAN

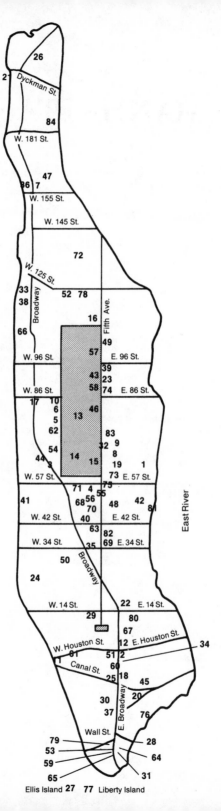

26

2 Dyckman St.

84

W. 181 St.

47
36 7
W. 155 St.

W. 145 St.

72

W. 125 St.
33   Broadway
38   52 78
66   16   Fifth Ave.
      49
      57   E. 96 St.
W. 96 St.
      39
      43   23
W. 86 St.   58   74   E. 86 St.
17 10
   6   13   46
   5
   62   83
   54   32 9
44 3   8
   14   15 19   1
W. 57 St.   73   E. 57 St.
      75
   71 4 55
   68 56
41   70   48   42
      40   81
W. 42 St.   E. 42 St.
      63
      82
W. 34 St.   35   69   E. 34 St.
   50
24   Broadway

W. 14 St.   22   E. 14 St.
   29   80
      67
      12   E. Houston St.
W. Houston St.   34
   81   51 2
   Canal St.   60
      25 18
      45
   30   E. Broadway   20
   37   76
Wall St.
79   28
53   64
59
65   31
Ellis Island 27   77 Liberty Island

Hudson River

East River

1 · ABIGAIL ADAMS SMITH MUSEUM

The Abigail Adams Smith Museum, established in 1939, is housed in what was once the carriage house (built in 1799) of the East River estate planned by Abigail Adams Smith and her husband, Colonel William Stephens Smith. The Smiths were prevented from completing the estate due to financial difficulties. After serving a later owner for a number of years as a private residence, this "Mount Vernon on the East River" was converted into a country hotel; in 1826, after fire destroyed the main building, the stone carriage house was remodeled and opened as the new Mount Vernon Hotel. Located five miles from the developed area of New York City, this establishment provided New Yorkers with an elegant country retreat. Today, the museum's renovated period rooms and furniture reflect what life was like in a nineteenth-century hotel.

Address/Telephone: 421 East 61 Street (between York and First Avenues), New York, NY 10021, (212) 838-6878

When to Visit: Mondays–Fridays—noon to 4 P.M. (Groups only—10 A.M. to noon) September–May: Mondays–Fridays—noon to 4 P.M. Sundays—1 P.M. to 5 P.M. June–July: Mondays–Fridays—noon to 4 P.M. Thursdays—evening programs

Days/Holidays Closed: August, Saturdays and holidays

Charges/Fees: Adults—$3; seniors, students—$2; children under 12—free

Suggested Grades: 4–6

Guided Tour: Yes; 40 to 45 minutes

Maximum Group: 35

Eating Facilities: None. Picnic facilities available in nearby parks

Restroom Facilities: Yes

Handicapped Access: Only to auditorium

Gift Shop: Yes

Library/Research Facilities: By appointment only

By Subway: N or R to Lexington Avenue; Nos. 4, 5 or 6 to 59 Street

By Bus: M15, M31 or M58

Additional Information: The museum has a regular schedule of concerts, lectures and other public programs; call for information. The museum also has special seasonal events.

2 · ALTERNATIVE MUSEUM

Founded in 1975, the Alternative Museum is a nonprofit, artist-administered institution offering issue-oriented exhibitions of humanitarian significance. Its exhibition program emphasizes individual artistic development and experimentation, and features the work of artists who have been disenfranchised because of ideology, race or gender. Each year the Alternative Museum produces five to seven panel discussions and lectures on diverse topics in the visual arts. Each season the museum presents 12 to 16 concerts of New Music, jazz, ethnic and experimental music.

Address/Telephone: Room 402, 594 Broadway, New York, NY 10012, (212) 966-4444

When to Visit: September–July: Tuesdays–Saturdays—11 A.M. to 6 P.M.

Days/Holidays Closed: August, Sundays and Mondays
Charges/Fees: Suggested donation—$3
Guided Tour: Brief tours for organized groups available on request
Group Notice: 1 week
Eating Facilities: None

Restroom Facilities: Yes
Handicapped Access: Yes
By Subway: N or R to Prince Street; No. 6 to Bleecker Street; B, D, F or Q to Broadway–Lafayette Street
By Bus: M1, M5 or M6

3 · AMERICAN BIBLE SOCIETY GALLERY AND LIBRARY

The American Bible Society houses an extensive library that includes nearly 50,000 Scripture items, dating from the thirteenth century to the present, in nearly 2000 languages and dialects. Its archives are a source of photographs, handwritten letters, printed sermons, oral-history recordings and materials documenting the history of the society itself. Among these materials are nineteenth-century correspondence with missionaries and biblical trans-lators in the Near East, Far East, Latin America and South America. The gallery mounts rotating exhibits and special presentations on the history of the Bible, including a replica of Johannes Gutenberg's press.

Address/Telephone: 12th floor, 1865 Broad-way, New York, NY 10023, (212) 408-1236
When to Visit: Mondays–Fridays—9 A.M. to 4:30 P.M.
Days/Holidays Closed: Saturdays, Sundays and major holidays
Charges/Fees: Free
Suggested Grades: 6–adult
Guided Tour: Yes
Maximum Group: 15

Group Notice: 2 weeks
Eating Facilities: None
Restroom Facilities: Yes
Handicapped Access: Yes
Gift Shop: Bookstore
Library/Research Facilities: Yes
By Subway: Nos. 1, 9, A, C, D or B (according to schedule) to 59 Street–Columbus Circle
By Bus: M5, M7, M10 or M104

4 · AMERICAN CRAFT MUSEUM

The museum was established in 1956 to collect, conserve, interpret, document and exhibit twentieth-century craft in the various media: wood, clay, fiber, metal, glass and plastic. The museum's exhibitions have a national and international focus, emphasizing craft's relation to design, architecture and the decorative arts. The collection includes contemporary American craft objects of high quality.

Address/Telephone: 40 West 53 Street, New York, NY 10019, (212) 956-3535

When to Visit: Tuesdays—10 A.M. to 8 P.M.
Wednesdays–Sundays—10 A.M. to 5 P.M.

Days/Holidays Closed: Mondays, New Year's Day, July 4, Thanksgiving and Christmas
Charges/Fees: Adults—$4.50; seniors, students—$2; members, children under 12—free
Suggested Grades: All grades
Guided Tour: Thursdays at 12:30 P.M., Saturdays at 11 and 11:30 A.M.
Maximum Group: 35
Group Notice: 4-week minimum
Eating Facilities: None
Restroom Facilities: Yes

Handicapped Access: Yes
Gift Shop: Yes
Library/Research Facilities: None
By Subway: E or F to Fifth Avenue; B, D, F or Q to 47–50 Streets–Rockefeller Center; Nos. 1 or 9 to 50 Street
By Bus: M1 or M5
Additional Information: Hands-on activities are available for children's group tours. Teachers should contact the Education Department, (212) 956-3535

5 · AMERICAN MUSEUM OF NATURAL HISTORY

Founded in 1869, the American Museum of Natural History is one of the world's preeminent science and research institutions, housing over 30 million artifacts and specimens. The museum possesses the most scientifically important collection of dinosaur fossils in existence and has been a leader in the study of these animals for nearly a century. The two recently renovated dinosaur halls contain over 100 dinosaur specimens, most of which are real (as opposed to casts), alongside the latest scientific information about these fascinating creatures. The Lila Acheson Wallace Wing of Mammals and Their Extinct Relatives, opened in 1994, is the largest collection of fossil mammals on display in the world. Two additional halls, the Hall of Vertebrate Origins and the Miriam and Ira D. Wallach Orientation Center, will open in 1996. Together, these six halls will illustrate the history of vertebrate evolution. A special program at the museum, "Expedition: Treasures from 125 Years of Discovery," allows visitors to chart their own course through 40 exhibition halls using a self-guided CD-ROM audio guide in search of 50 of the museum's most intriguing treasures. The Hall of Human Biology and Evolution traces the complex pattern of human evolution and the origins of creation through fossil exhibits, life-size dioramas of early hominids, holographic models and interactive technology. The museum also features well-known animal habitat dioramas, anthropological collections, the Hall of Ocean Life, the Hall of Minerals and Gems, meteorites and the Naturemax Theater, where IMAX films are presented daily.

Address/Telephone: Central Park West at 79 Street, New York, NY 10024, (212) 769-5100
When to Visit: Sundays–Thursdays—10 A.M. to 5:45 P.M., Fridays–Saturdays—10 A.M. to 8:45 P.M.

Days/Holidays Closed: Thanksgiving and Christmas
Charges/Fees: Suggested donations: adults—$6; seniors, students—$4; children—$3
Suggested Grades: All grades

Guided Tour: Free highlights tours offered daily; 1 hour, 15 minutes
Maximum Group: Unlimited
Group Notice: Call for reservations
Eating Facilities: Yes (Garden Café restaurant and Diner Saurus snack bar)
Restroom Facilities: Yes

Handicapped Access: Yes
Gift Shop: Yes
Library/Research Facilities: Yes
By Subway: B (according to schedule) or C to 81 Street; Nos. 1 or 9 to 79 Street
By Bus: M7, M10, M11, M79 or M104

The American Museum–Hayden Planetarium.

6 · AMERICAN MUSEUM–
HAYDEN PLANETARIUM

The Hayden Planetarium (the Department of Astronomy of the American Museum of Natural History) was opened to the public in 1935. Since then, the planetarium has been visited by more than 30 million people. The focal point of the planetarium is the Sky Theater—one of the world's largest sky theaters, seating 650. Daily Sky Shows as well as school presentations on various topics in astronomy are offered; on Friday and Saturday evenings, the theater presents a laser-light show. The planetarium offers a variety of permanent exhibits, such as the Hall of the Sun, antique astronomical instruments, art displays and the Black Light Gallery featuring glowing murals on space-related topics. The Guggenheim Space Theater features wrap-around slide presentations (on 22 screens) that serve primarily as an introduction to the Sky Shows.

Address/Telephone: Central Park West at West 81 Street, New York, NY 10024, (212) 769-5100

When to Visit: October–June: Mondays–Fridays—12:30 P.M. to 4:45 P.M. Saturdays—10 A.M. to 5:45 P.M. Sundays—noon to 5:45 P.M. July–September: Mondays–Fridays—12:30 P.M. to 4:45 P.M. Saturdays–Sundays—noon to 4:45 P.M.

Days/Holidays Closed: Thanksgiving and Christmas

Charges/Fees: Adults—$5; seniors, students (with ID)—$4; children (2–12)—$2.50

Suggested Grades: Special weekday programs available for preschool through high-school groups

Guided Tour: None

Eating Facilities: Yes. Restaurant and cafeteria in the American Museum of Natural History, adjacent to the Hayden Planetarium. Picnic facilities available in Central Park

Restroom Facilities: Yes

Handicapped Access: Yes (ramp entrance through parking lot on West 81 Street; elevator available)

Gift Shop: Yes

Library/Research Facilities: Yes

By Subway: B (according to schedule) or C to 81 Street; Nos. 1 or 9 to 79 Street

By Bus: M7, M10, M11, M79 or M104

7 · AMERICAN NUMISMATIC SOCIETY

The American Numismatic Society was founded in 1858 to facilitate the study of money. Housed in the landmark Audubon Terrace complex, the society maintains a collection of more than one million objects—coins, paper money, medals and related items. The society's reference library contains more than 100,000 volumes. In addition to exhibiting its collection, the society offers a number of outreach programs and mounts traveling exhibits that circulate to schools, libraries and coin conventions.

Address/Telephone: Broadway at West 155 Street (between West 155 and 156 Streets), New York, NY 10032, (212) 234-3130
When to Visit: Tuesdays–Saturdays—9:30 A.M. to 4:30 P.M. Sundays–1 P.M. to 4 P.M.
Days/Holidays Closed: Mondays, New Year's Day, July 4, Labor Day, Thanksgiving and Christmas
Charges/Fees: Free
Suggested Grades: 6–adult
Guided Tour: Yes; 30 minutes

Maximum Group: 30
Group Notice: 2 weeks
Eating Facilities: None. Limited picnic facilities on terrace
Restroom Facilities: Yes
Handicapped Access: None
Gift Shop: Small shop selling cards and medals
Library/Research Facilities: Yes
By Subway: Nos. 1 or 9 to West 157 Street
By Bus: M4, M5, M100, M101 or Bx6

8 · AMERICAS SOCIETY

The Americas Society is dedicated to informing people in the United States about the societies and cultures of neighboring peoples of the Western Hemisphere. Its Visual Arts Department has an active exhibition and publication program that presents the diverse artistic traditions of Latin America, Canada and the Caribbean to audiences in New York and throughout the United States. In conjunction with each exhibition, a comprehensive education program of lectures, symposia, gallery tours, teacher workshops and community-outreach activities is organized. The library houses a resource collection of art books, monographs, magazines and an archive containing biographical and bibliographical documentation and slides of more than 4000 artists from the Americas.

Address/Telephone: 680 Park Avenue (at East 68 Street), New York, NY 10021, (212) 249-8950
When to Visit: Exhibition hours: Tuesdays–Sundays—noon to 6 P.M.
Days/Holidays Closed: Sundays, Mondays, New Year's Day, Thanksgiving and the following day, Christmas and all other major holidays
Charges/Fees: Suggested donation—$3
Suggested Grades: 4–adult
Guided Tour: 1-hour tours available to groups by appointment
Maximum Group: 50

Group Notice: 1 month
Eating Facilities: None. Picnic facilities in nearby Central Park
Restroom Facilities: Yes
Handicapped Access: Yes
Gift Shop: Sales desk offering exhibition catalogs
Library/Research Facilities: By appointment only (open to scholars, critics, students and curators)
By Subway: No. 6 to 68 Street (walk one block west to Park and East 68 Street)
By Bus: M1, M2, M3, M4 or M66

9 · ASIA SOCIETY

The Asia Society mounts imaginative exhibitions of ancient and modern art assembled from public and private collections in Asia and the West, as well as masterpieces from the society's permanent collection, the Mr. and

Mrs. John D. Rockefeller 3rd Collection of Asian Art. These exhibitions travel to museums throughout the United States and Asia. In recent years the society has launched a major new program to present contemporary Asian and Asian-American art, with the help of leading scholars, curators and critics in Asia and the United States. The society also presents public programs, films, lectures and performances, and publishes exhibition catalogues and a journal on Asian art.

Address/Telephone: 725 Park Avenue (at East 70 Street), New York, NY 10021, (212) 288-6400 (or 517-ASIA)

When to Visit: Tuesdays, Wednesdays, Fridays and Saturdays 11 A.M. to 6 P.M. Thursdays— 11 A.M. to 8 P.M. Sundays—noon to 5 P.M.

Days/Holidays Closed: Mondays and all major holidays

Charges/Fees: Adults—$3; seniors, students— $1; members and children under 12 (with parent)—free

Guided Tour: Gallery talks, Tuesdays–Saturdays, 12:30 P.M. Thursdays, 12:30 P.M. and 6:30 P.M. Sundays, 2:30 P.M.

Eating Facilities: None

Restroom Facilities: Yes

Handicapped Access: Yes

Gift Shop: Yes

By Subway: No. 6 to 68 Street

By Bus: M1, M2, M3, M4, M18, M30, M66, M72, M101 or M102

10 · BARD GRADUATE CENTER FOR STUDIES IN THE DECORATIVE ARTS

Located in a turn-of-the-century Beaux-Arts town house, the center's exhibitions are set off by the most distinctive architectural design elements of the early twentieth century—a winding staircase, elaborate moldings, paneling and plaster work, marble and plaster mantelpieces and floral-patterned stained-glass windows. Exhibitions feature the decorative arts of various periods and cultures. The Bard Center also offers a variety of public courses, seminars and lectures, as well as gallery tours and architectural walking tours of New York City.

Address/Telephone: 18 West 86 Street (between Central Park West and Columbus Avenue), New York, NY 10024, (212) 501-3000

When to Visit: Tuesdays, Wednesdays, Fridays– Sundays—11 A.M. to 5 P.M. Thursdays—11 A.M. to 8:30 P.M.

Days/Holidays Closed: Mondays

Charges/Fees: Adults—$2; seniors—$1; children under 12—free

Suggested Grades: Contact Public Programs, (212) 721-4977, for information on school programs

Guided Tour: Yes. Call Public Programs for more information, (212) 721-4977

Maximum Group: Depends on program

Group Notice: Depends on program

Eating Facilities: None

Restroom Facilities: Yes

Handicapped Access: Yes

Bard Graduate Center for Studies in the Decorative Arts.
(Photograph by Durston Saylor)

Gift Shop: Catalogs available
Library/Research Facilities: By appointment only

By Subway: B (according to schedule) or C to West 86 Street
By Bus: M10 or M86

• CARNEGIE HALL: *see* ROSE MUSEUM AT CARNEGIE HALL

11 • CASTILLO CULTURAL CENTER

A multicultural arts center, Castillo strives to create an environment in which artists, actors, writers, psychologists, educators and activists can unite to experiment with new artistic forms. At Castillo, people are encouraged to do what they do not know how to do, and become doers and creators of new approaches to art, theater, music, philosophy and psychology.

Address/Telephone: Second floor, 500 Greenwich Street (between Spring and Canal Streets), New York, NY 10013, (212) 941-5800

When to Visit: Mondays–Fridays—10 A.M. to 10 P.M. Saturdays and Sundays—noon to 10 P.M.

Days/Holidays Closed: New Year's Day, July 4, Labor Day, Memorial Day and Christmas

Charges/Fees: Free

Suggested Grades: 6–adult

Guided Tour: Yes; approximately 20 minutes

Maximum Group: 10

Group Notice: 24 hours (if possible)

Eating Facilities: Yes (café open during theater performances)

Restroom Facilities: Yes

Handicapped Access: Yes

Gift Shop: None

Library/Research Facilities: None

By Subway: Nos. 1 or 9 to Houston Street; C or E to Spring Street

By Bus: M10, M21

12 · CENTER FOR BOOK ARTS

The Center for Book Arts is a nonprofit arts organization dedicated to the preservation of traditional bookmaking crafts as well as the contemporary interpretations of the book as an art object. In addition to providing a work space for artists in a fully-equipped print shop and bindery, the center offers exhibitions of established and emerging book artists and educational courses in traditional and contemporary bookbinding, letterpress printing and papermaking.

Address/Telephone: Fifth floor, 626 Broadway (between Bleecker and East Houston Streets), New York, NY 10012, (212) 460-9768

When to Visit: Mondays–Fridays—10 A.M. to 6 P.M. Saturdays—10 A.M. to 4 P.M.

Days/Holidays Closed: Sundays, New Year's Day, Memorial Day, July 4, Labor Day, Thanksgiving and Christmas

Charges/Fees: Free

Suggested Grades: 6–adult

Guided Tour: Yes (informal tours by staff; more detailed tours with demonstrations available)

Maximum Group: 25–30

Group Notice: 1–2 weeks

Eating Facilities: None

Restroom Facilities: Yes

Handicapped Access: Limited

Gift Shop: Books available for sale

Library/Research Facilities: Modest collection of literature on books

By Subway: N or R to Prince Street; B, D, F or Q to Broadway-Lafayette Street; No. 6 to Bleecker Street

By Bus: M5 or M6

13 · CENTRAL PARK, BELVEDERE CASTLE

Located in mid-Central Park, this medieval-style structure, designed by Calvert Vaux, one of the park's creators, is home to the urban park rangers. Belvedere Castle also serves as the National Weather Service Station for New York City. Visitors have access to an upstairs terrace for viewing—the highest manmade observation point in the park. Belvedere Castle has permanent exhibits relating to geology, park history, weather and birds.

Address/Telephone: Mid-park at 80 Street, Central Park, New York, NY, (212) 772-0210

Mailing Address: The Arsenal, Central Park, Attn: Belvedere Castle, New York, NY 10021

When to Visit: Wednesdays and Thursdays—11 A.M. to 5 P.M. Fridays—1 P.M. to 4 P.M. Saturdays and Sundays—11 A.M. to 5 P.M.

Days/Holidays Closed: Mondays and Tuesdays

Charges/Fees: Free

Suggested Grades: All grades

Guided Tour: There is no tour of the castle itself, but rangers run various park tours

Eating Facilities: None. Picnic facilities available in Central Park

Restroom Facilities: None

Handicapped Access: None

Gift Shop: Small gift shop

Library/Research Facilities: None

By Subway: C or B (according to schedule) to West 81 Street

By Bus: M10 or M79

14 · CENTRAL PARK, THE DAIRY

One of the park's original structures, the Dairy housed a herd of milk cows. Today, bereft of livestock, it features a modest exhibit on Central Park's historical development. It also features an interactive video with points of interest throughout the park and has a 12-foot three-dimensional map of the park as well as a selection of books and maps about Central Park available for purchase.

Address/Telephone: Mid-park at 64 Street (west of Central Park Zoo, east of the carousel), Central Park, (212) 794-6564

Mailing Address: The Dairy, 830 Fifth Avenue, New York, NY 10021

When to Visit: Mid-February–mid-October: Tuesdays–Sundays—11 A.M. to 5 P.M. Mid-October–mid-February: Tuesdays–Sundays—11 A.M. to 4 P.M.

Charges/Fees: Free

Suggested Grades: All grades

Guided Tour: None

Maximum Group: Children's groups must be chaperoned; no more than 20 children at once

Eating Facilities: None. Limited picnic facilities available; no barbecuing

Restroom Facilities: None

Handicapped Access: Yes

Gift Shop: Small gift shop

Library/Research Facilities: Small resource library

By Subway: N or R to Fifth Avenue

By Bus: M1, M2, M3, M4 or M5

15 · CENTRAL PARK WILDLIFE CENTER (CENTRAL PARK ZOO)

The zoo is a part of the Wildlife Conservation Society, founded in 1895 as the New York Zoological Society. Located on five and a half acres in Central Park, the Central Park Wildlife Center is home to approximately 450 animals of over 100 species. The zoo is divided into three climatic zones: the Tropic Zone, the Temperate Territory and the Polar Circle. The Tropic Zone is a skylighted building containing a simulated tropical forest with an open aviary for tropical birds and bats. Visitors can stroll along two levels of viewing areas to catch glimpses of brightly colored exotic birds. Inside they can peer through plate-glass windows to watch a variety of tropical forest life, from leaf-cutter ants to Amazonian tree frogs and snakes. The Temperate Territory's environments include a lake with an island of Japanese snow monkeys, a central garden and a sea-lion pool. The Polar Circle's main attraction are the polar bears in their naturalistic setting. Ten separate viewing areas, including above- and below-water areas, allow visitors to watch the bears swim. Other polar animals include arctic foxes and, inside the Edge of the Ice Pack building, penguins and tufted puffins. In addition to the animals at the Wildlife Center there is also a Wildlife Gallery with changing exhibitions of art on animal-related themes. The Zoo School features two classrooms and an auditorium for programs on wildlife education for children and adults.

Address/Telephone: 830 Fifth Avenue (at 64 Street), New York, NY 10021, (212) 439-6500

When to Visit: April–October: Mondays–Fridays—10 A.M. to 5 P.M. Saturdays, Sundays and holidays—10 A.M. to 5:30 P.M. November–March: daily—10 A.M. to 4:30 P.M.

Charges/Fees: Adults—$2.50; seniors—$1.25; children (3–12)—$.50; children under 3—free

Suggested Grades: All grades

Guided Tour: Informal tours offered daily, once a day; 1 hour

Maximum Group: No maximum

Group Notice: None required

Eating Facilities: Yes

Restroom Facilities: Yes

Handicapped Access: Yes

Gift Shop: Yes

Library/Research Facilities: None

By Subway: N or R to Fifth Avenue; No. 6 to 68 Street

By Bus: M1, M2, M3, M4, M18, M30, M66 or M72

Additional Information: Call the Education Department for more information about the Zoo School

16 · CHARLES A. DANA DISCOVERY CENTER

Opened in 1993, the center features a permanent exhibit of "The Fragile Forest"—an educational guide to the forest's ecosystem—and a hands-on science exhibit. The Discovery Center sits on the Harlem Meer—a lake at the north end of Central Park—and supplies bait and fishing poles (free with picture ID) in the summer. Family workshops are offered on weekends, and the Harlem Meer Performance Festival—featuring local musicians—is held every Saturday afternoon from May to August.

Address/Telephone: 36 West 110 Street (at Fifth Avenue), New York, NY 10026, (212) 860-1370

When to Visit: Tuesdays–Sundays—11 A.M. to 5 P.M.

Days/Holidays Closed: Mondays

Charges/Fees: Free

Suggested Grades: K–5

Guided Tour: None (park rangers provide outdoor walking tours)

Eating Facilities: None. Limited picnic facilities available
Restroom Facilities: Yes
Handicapped Access: Yes

Gift Shop: None
Library/Research Facilities: None
By Subway: Nos. 2 or 3 to 110 Street
By Bus: M1, M2, M3, M4 or M18

17 · CHILDREN'S MUSEUM OF MANHATTAN

The museum welcomes nearly 250,000 children and their families each year. In addition to a variety of temporary exhibits, the museum houses several permanent activity centers, including two family play areas: the Family Learning Center, designed for families with children under six to play together creatively; and the Early Childhood Center, designed for families with children under four. The Early Childhood Center is part of the Time Warner Center for Media, the Performing Arts and Early Childhood Education, which also features a full-scale television-production studio in which children can participate, and a performance space with stage and rehearsal area and audience seating for 200. The Sussman Environmental Center is an outdoor exhibit housing the Urban Tree House, a three-story steel structure in which children explore environmental issues through interactive displays and activities.

Address/Telephone: The Tisch Building, 212 West 83 Street (between Broadway and Amsterdam Avenue), New York, NY 10024, (212) 721-1234
When to Visit: Mondays, Wednesdays, Thursdays—1:30 P.M. to 5:30 P.M. Fridays, Saturdays, Sundays, summer and school holidays—10 A.M. to 5 P.M.
Days/Holidays Closed: Tuesdays, New Year's Day, Labor Day and Christmas
Charges/Fees: Adults, children—$5; seniors—$2.50; children under 2—free

Suggested Grades: All grades
Guided Tour: None
Eating Facilities: None
Restroom Facilities: Yes
Handicapped Access: Yes
Gift Shop: Yes
Library/Research Facilities: Yes
By Subway: Nos. 1 or 9 to 86 Street; B (according to schedule) or C to 81 Street or to 86 Street
By Bus: M86 or M104

18 · CHILDREN'S MUSEUM OF THE ARTS

The Children's Museum of the Arts provides interactive arts programs and exhibitions for children aged 18 months to ten years and their families. Permanent exhibits include the "International Children's Art Gallery," in which the museum displays approximately 100 artworks by children throughout the world (part of a 2000-piece collection). The Monet Ball Pond and Magnetic Masterpieces are among the interactive exhibits for children. Through The Artist Studio and The Wee Studio, the museum offers daily art workshops that instruct children in various media, such as paint, collage, sand painting and origami. Special afterschool arts workshops and weekend workshops are also available.

Address/Telephone: 72 Spring Street (between Broadway and Lafayette Street), New York, NY 10012, (212) 274-0986

When to Visit: Tuesdays–Sundays—11 A.M. to 5 P.M.

Days/Holidays Closed: Mondays, New Year's Day, Easter, Memorial Day, Thanksgiving and Christmas

Charges/Fees: Tuesdays–Fridays—$4, Saturdays and Sundays—$5

Suggested Grades: K–5

Maximum Group: 30 children

Group Notice: 2 weeks–1 month (depending on time of year)

Eating Facilities: None

Restroom Facilities: Yes

Handicapped Access: Yes

Gift Shop: Yes

Library/Research Facilities: None

By Subway: No. 6 to Spring Street; B, D, F or Q to Broadway–Lafayette Street; N or R to Prince Street

By Bus: M1, M5 or M6

19 · CHINA INSTITUTE GALLERY

Founded in 1966, the China Institute Gallery is located in a historic town house on New York's Upper East Side. The gallery presents two major exhibitions a year, along with a smaller annual Chinese New Year's show. Working closely with museums in China and the United States, the gallery is able to borrow from collections otherwise inaccessible to most Americans. It also sponsors trips to China and offers symposia, lecture series and other educational programs promoting Chinese art and culture.

Address/Telephone: 125 East 65 Street (between Lexington and Park Avenues), New York, NY 10021, (212) 744-8181

When to Visit: Mondays, Wednesdays–Saturdays—10 A.M. to 5 P.M. Tuesdays—10 A.M. to 8 P.M. Sundays—1 P.M. to 5 P.M.

Days/Holidays Closed: New Year's Day, Chinese New Year, July 4, Thanksgiving and Christmas

Charges/Fees: Suggested donation—$5

Suggested Grades: All grades

Guided Tour: By appointment only; 30 minutes

Maximum Group: 30

Group Notice: 3 weeks

Eating Facilities: None

Restroom Facilities: Yes

Handicapped Access: None

Gift Shop: Yes (Exhibition catalogues and small gift items only)

Library/Research Facilities: None

By Subway: No. 6 to 68 Street; B or Q (according to schedule) to Lexington Avenue

By Bus: M1, M2, M3, M4, M101 or M102

20 · CHINATOWN HISTORY MUSEUM

Founded in 1980, the museum houses the country's most extensive research collection of oral histories, personal letters, documents, photographs, memorabilia and other artifacts relating to the Chinese experience in America. Housed on the second floor of a public school at the corner of Mulberry and Bayard Streets, the museum works to preserve the heritage of Chinese immigrants through exhibitions and education. The Resource Bank provides information on almost all elements of Chinatown history— local industry, economics and other cultural topics. The museum's gallery mounts temporary exhibits of works by Chinese artists. Organized walking tours around Chinatown are also offered.

Address/Telephone: Second floor, 70 Mulberry Street, New York, NY 10013, (212) 619-4785

When to Visit: Sundays–Fridays—noon to 5 P.M.

Days/Holidays Closed: Saturdays, New Year's Day, Martin Luther King, Jr.'s Birthday, Chinese Lunar New Year, Presidents' Day, Easter, Memorial Day, July 4, Labor Day, Thanksgiving and Christmas

Charges/Fees: Adults—$1; children—free

Suggested Grades: 3–adult

Guided Tour: By appointment only

Group Notice: 2-week minimum

Eating Facilities: None

Restroom Facilities: Yes

Handicapped Access: None

Gift Shop: Yes, and small bookstore

Library/Research Facilities: By appointment only

By Subway: N, R, J, M, Z or No. 6 to Canal Street

By Bus: M9, M15, M101 or M102

Additional Information: At press time, the museum was closed for renovation; it is scheduled to reopen sometime in Fall 1995

· CLOCKTOWER GALLERY: see INSTITUTE FOR CONTEMPORARY ART

21 · THE CLOISTERS

A branch of the Metropolitan Museum of Art, The Cloisters is devoted to the architecture and art of medieval Europe. Located high on a hilltop overlooking the Hudson River, its modern structure, built in a medieval style, incorporates chapels, sections of monastic cloisters, a chapter house and other architectural elements dating from the twelfth through the fifteenth centuries. On view are medieval sculptures, tapestries (including the famous Unicorn Tapestries), paintings, illuminated manuscripts, metalwork and stained glass. Other highlights include flower and herb gardens, featuring more than 250 species of plants cultivated in the Middle Ages.

The Cloisters. *(The Metropolitan Museum of Art, The Cloisters Collection)*

Address/Telephone: Fort Tryon Park, New York, NY 10040, (212) 923-3700

When to Visit: March–October: Tuesdays–Sundays—9:30 A.M. to 5:15 P.M. November–February: Tuesdays–Sundays—9:30 A.M. to 4:45 P.M.

Days/Holidays Closed: Mondays, New Year's Day, Thanksgiving and Christmas

Charges/Fees: Suggested donations: adults—$7; seniors, students—$3.50; children under 12 with an adult—free

Suggested Grades: All grades

Guided Tour: Tuesdays–Fridays at 3 P.M., Sundays at noon; 45 minutes to 1 hour

Maximum Group: 30

Eating Facilities: None. Picnic facilities available in Fort Tryon Park
Restroom Facilities: Yes
Handicapped Access: Partial
Gift Shop: Yes
Library/Research Facilities: By appointment only
By Subway: A to 190 Street (exit via elevator; 10-minute walk through Fort Tryon Park)
By Bus: M4, M100 or Bx7
Additional Information: The park is at the northern end of Ft. Washington Avenue; the last cross street is West 190 Street; this is about 1 mile north of George Washington Bridge. Special Events: gallery talks and demonstrations on Saturdays; medieval concerts and dramas on selected Sundays (October–May)

22 · CON EDISON ENERGY MUSEUM

The museum houses a unique collection tracing the history and future of electricity as a source of energy. Many of the exhibits present Thomas Edison's life and works, including a model of the inventor's Pearl Street power plant and the complete system—dynamos, regulators, meters and other apparatus—he developed to "light up" New York City's first district with electricity. A film incorporating historical photographs shows New York at the turn of the century and the ways in which electricity changed people's lives. One of the museum's most popular exhibits features a simulated walking tour beneath a typical New York City street where visitors can see colorfully illuminated utility lines and watch a passing subway. Exhibits also focus on current research and development in nuclear energy and energy conservation.

Address/Telephone: 145 East 14 Street (at Third Avenue), New York, NY 10003, (212) 460-6244
When to Visit: Tuesdays–Saturdays—9 A.M. to 5 P.M.
Days/Holidays Closed: Sundays, Mondays and all major holidays (call for more information)
Charges/Fees: Free
Suggested Grades: All grades
Guided Tour: Yes; 1 hour
Maximum Group: 36
Group Notice: As far in advance as possible
Eating Facilities: None
Restroom Facilities: Yes
Handicapped Access: Yes
Gift Shop: None
Library/Research Facilities: None
By Subway: L, N, R, Nos. 4, 5 or 6 to 14 Street–Union Square
By Bus: M9, M14, M101 or M102
Additional Information: To arrange for school or community group tours, call (212) 460-6244

23 · COOPER-HEWITT NATIONAL DESIGN MUSEUM

The Cooper-Hewitt National Design Museum (a division of the Smithsonian Institution) is housed in the landmark Andrew Carnegie mansion of 1901. The museum's nearly 250,000 works include drawings and prints, rare books, textiles, wall coverings, furniture, ceramics, glass, metalwork and jewelry. The collections are international, include both historic and contemporary design, and range from one-of-a-kind to mass-produced items. In addition to the gallery, the museum provides educational programs for children and adults, lectures, seminars, workshops, tours and gallery talks. The Doris & Henry Dreyfull Study Center contains more than 50,000 volumes, a picture library of over one million images and an archive of twentieth-century design works.

Address/Telephone: 2 East 91 Street (at Fifth Avenue), New York, NY 10128, (212) 860-6868

When to Visit: Tuesdays—10 A.M. to 9 P.M. Wednesdays–Saturdays—10 A.M. to 5 P.M. Sundays—noon to 5 P.M.

Days/Holidays Closed: Mondays and all federal holidays

Charges/Fees: General admission—$3; seniors, students—$1.50; museum and Smithsonian members and children under 12—free

Suggested Grades: All grades

Guided Tour: Yes

Maximum Group: 20

Group Notice: As far in advance as possible (2-week minimum)

Eating Facilities: None

Restroom Facilities: Yes

Handicapped Access: Yes

Gift Shop: Yes

Library/Research Facilities: By appointment only

By Subway: Nos. 4, 5 or 6 to 86 Street

By Bus: M1, M2, M3, M4, M18, M19, M86 or M96

24 · DIA CENTER FOR THE ARTS

In 1987, Dia opened an exhibition facility in a four-story renovated warehouse. The program at this facility is principally dedicated to large-scale, single-artist projects. Exhibitions are long-term, usually with a minimum duration of one year, to allow viewers the opportunity to see the work over an extended period of time. Past exhibitions have included works by Joseph Beuys, Jenny Holzer, Brice Marden and Francesco Clemente. Works from Dia's permanent collection are also presented from time to time. In addition, Dia offers an Art Education Program to introduce junior-high-school teachers and students to contemporary visual art and poetry through museum visits, lectures and studio workshops.

Address/Telephone: 548 West 22 Street, New York, NY, (212) 431-9232

Mailing Address: 155 Mercer Street, New York, NY 10012

When to Visit: Thursdays–Sundays—noon to 6 P.M.

Days/Holidays Closed: August and Mondays–Wednesdays

Charges/Fees: Free

Suggested Grades: All grades

Guided Tour: By appointment only

Eating Facilities: Yes (snack bar)

Restroom Facilities: Yes

Handicapped Access: Yes

Gift Shop: Yes

Library/Research Facilities: None

By Subway: C or E to 23 Street

By Bus: M10, M11 or M23

Additional Information: Dia also operates facilities at 393 West Broadway and 141

Wooster Street (call for exhibition information). The Printed Matter Bookstore at Dia (77 Wooster Street, Tuesdays–Saturdays, 10 A.M. to 6 P.M.) sells and distributes selected artists' books and publications related to Dia's programs

25 • DRAWING CENTER

The Drawing Center focuses on the exhibition of drawings, both contemporary and historical; at least one historical exhibit is mounted a year. Four to five contemporary exhibitions are mounted annually, including "Selections," a series of group shows of artists chosen by the center's curatorial staff. The center regularly presents readings, lectures, panels, performances and paper-construction workshops, as well as a comprehensive school program for students K–12, which includes a drawing class.

Address/Telephone: 35 Wooster Street (between Broome and Grand Streets), New York, NY 10013, (212) 219-2166

When to Visit: Tuesdays, Thursdays and Fridays—10 A.M. to 6 P.M. Wednesdays—10 A.M. to 8 P.M. Saturdays—11 A.M. to 6 P.M.

Days/Holidays Closed: Sundays, Mondays, August and December 25–January 1

Charges/Fees: Free except for historical exhibitions, when the center requests donations

Suggested Grades: All grades (call for information on education programs)

Guided Tour: By appointment only; 30–45 minutes

Maximum Group: 25

Group Notice: 1 month

Eating Facilities: None

Restroom Facilities: Yes

Handicapped Access: Yes

Gift Shop: Bookstore featuring the Drawing Center's publications

Library/Research Facilities: Yes

By Subway: Nos. 1, 9, A, C, E, N or R to Canal Street

By Bus: M1, M6 or M10

26 • DYCKMAN FARMHOUSE MUSEUM

In 1661, Jan Dyckman arrived in New York from Westphalia and purchased several acres of remote land in northern Manhattan. He and his descendants expanded their landholdings until the farmhouse was the center of one of the largest estates in Manhattan's history—some 450 acres at its peak. During the Revolutionary War, the British occupied the house and burned it. The present Dutch-American–style house was built by Dyckman's grandson, William, in 1784 and it remained in the family until the 1800s. Today, Dyckman House is Manhattan's last surviving Colonial farmhouse. The house contains English and early American Colonial furnishings, including a Bible and a cradle once used by Dyckman family members. Relics from the Revolutionary War include pottery fragments, flint-tips, kitchen utensils and a replica of a military hut that has been reconstructed near its original site in the garden.

Address/Telephone: 4881 Broadway (at West 204 Street), New York, NY 10034, (212) 304-9422

When to Visit: Tuesdays–Saturdays—11 A.M. to 4 P.M. (Due to limited staffing, please call prior to visiting)

Days/Holidays Closed: Most city, state and federal holidays. (Call prior to visiting)

Charges/Fees: Donation suggested

Suggested Grades: 5–adult

Guided Tour: Available upon request; approximately 1 hour

Maximum Group: 20

Group Notice: 2 weeks

Eating Facilities: None. Picnic facilities available

Restroom Facilities: Yes

Handicapped Access: None

Gift Shop: None

Library/Research Facilities: None

By Subway: A to 207 Street

By Bus: M100, Bx7, Bx12 or Bx20

Additional Information: Call the museum for information on special events

27 · ELLIS ISLAND IMMIGRATION MUSEUM

The museum has three floors of exhibits and audiovisual displays on American immigration history and on Ellis Island's history as an immigration station. There are more than 30 galleries filled with artifacts, historic photos, posters, maps, recorded oral histories and ethnic music. The National Park Service provides public tours; an audio-tour can be rented to enhance self-guided tours. There are also two theater facilities, each presenting a half-hour documentary film entitled "Island of Hope, Island of Tears"; in one theater, the film is accompanied by a 15-minute introductory talk. The NYNEX Learning Center, a half-hour interactive video program especially recommended for school groups and younger visitors, is also open daily. The American Immigrant Wall of Honor, memorializing 420,000 individual immigrants to America, is the largest wall of names in the world.

Address/Telephone: Ellis Island, New York, NY 10004, (212) 363-3200

When to Visit: Daily—9:15 A.M. to 5:30 P.M. (Extended hours during the summer)

Days/Holidays Closed: Christmas

Charges/Fees: There is no charge to enter the museum, but there is a charge for the ferry, operated by the Circle Line, (212) 269-5755. Round-trip fares: adults—$7; seniors—$5; children under 17—$3

Suggested Grades: All grades

Guided Tour: A variety of school programs are available. Call Educational Programs at (212) 363-7620

Maximum Group: Depends on program

Group Notice: Depends on program

Eating Facilities: Yes

Restroom Facilities: Yes

Handicapped Access: Yes

Gift Shop: Yes

Library/Research Facilities: By appointment only

By Subway: Nos. 1 or 9 to South Ferry; N or R to Whitehall Street; Nos. 4 or 5 to Bowling Green

By Bus: M1, M6 or M15

• FASHION INSTITUTE OF TECHNOLOGY: *see* MUSEUM AT
THE FASHION INSTITUTE OF TECHNOLOGY

Federal Hall National Memorial. *(National Park Service; photograph by Richard Frear)*

28 · FEDERAL HALL NATIONAL MEMORIAL

In the first building on this site—the old city hall, built in 1699–1701—the government of the United States began to function under our present Constitution and George Washington was sworn into office as President. From 1789 to 1790, the newly formed federal government was housed in the old city hall; by 1800 the government had moved to Washington, D.C., and Federal Hall (as it had come to be called) was no longer large enough to serve even New York City's needs. By the time a new (and current) City Hall was completed in 1812, Federal Hall had fallen into ruin and was sold for salvage. The building that now occupies the site was completed in 1842, a fine example of Greek Revival architecture. First used as the U.S. Customs building, then occupied by other governmental agencies, the structure and land were later designated a national historic site. Today various exhibits depicting the roles this site has played in American history are mounted there.

Address/Telephone: 26 Wall Street (at Nassau Street), New York, NY 10005, (212) 825-6888

When to Visit: Mondays–Fridays—9 A.M. to 5 P.M.

Days/Holidays Closed: Saturdays, Sundays and all federal holidays *except* July 4

Charges/Fees: Free

Suggested Grades: 3–adult

Guided Tour: Yes; 30 minutes

Maximum Group: 40

Group Notice: 2 weeks

Eating Facilities: None

Restroom Facilities: Yes

Handicapped Access: Yes

Gift Shop: None

Library/Research Facilities: None

By Subway: Nos. 2, 3, 4 or 5 to Wall Street; Nos. 1, 9, N or R to Rector Street; J, M or Z to Broad Street

By Bus: M1, M6 or M15

29 · FORBES MAGAZINE GALLERIES

The galleries are located on the main floor of the Forbes Building, built in 1925 and designed by the renowned architectural firm of Carrère & Hastings. Gallery exhibitions are drawn from the extensive collections begun by *Forbes Magazine* publisher Malcolm Forbes. Among the most famous are: "Toy Boats & Toy Soldiers" and "Important American Historical Papers," which includes George Washington's handwritten reminiscences of his military career, Paul Revere's expense account for his famous ride and Harry Truman's irate response to a reporter's criticism of his daughter's singing. "The World of Fabergé," with over 300 objets d'art, is perhaps the most famous of the exhibits, featuring eight Imperial Easter eggs created by Peter Carl Fabergé. The galleries also offer changing exhibitions of paintings, photographs and other works of art.

Address/Telephone: 62 Fifth Avenue (at 12 Street), New York, NY 10011, (212) 206-5548
When to Visit: Tuesdays–Saturdays—10 A.M. to 4 P.M.
Days/Holidays Closed: Sundays, Mondays and all legal holidays
Charges/Fees: Free
Suggested Grades: All grades (children under 16 must be accompanied by an adult)
Guided Tour: Yes

Maximum Group: 30
Group Notice: 2 weeks
Eating Facilities: None
Restroom Facilities: Yes
Handicapped Access: Yes
Gift Shop: None
Library/Research Facilities: None
By Subway: Nos. 4, 5, 6, L, N, R to 14 Street–Union Square; N or R to 8 Street; F to 14 Street
By Bus: M2, M3, M5, M6, M7, M14 or M18

30 · FRANKLIN FURNACE ARCHIVE, INC.

Franklin Furnace was originally founded to collect, catalog, conserve and exhibit contemporary artist-produced books and multiples. In 1993, the collection and archives were acquired by The Museum of Modern Art and merged with MoMA's own holdings, the combined collections forming one of the largest in the country. In addition to maintaining and expanding this resource, Franklin Furnace regularly organizes scholarly and historical exhibitions, emphasizes performance art and sponsors educational programs for local schoolchildren.

Address/Telephone: 112 Franklin Street (between Church Street and Broadway), New York, NY 10013, (212) 925-4671
When to Visit: Tuesdays–Saturdays—noon to 6 P.M.
Days/Holidays Closed: Mondays and all major holidays
Charges/Fees: Free

Guided Tour: None
Eating Facilities: None
Restroom Facilities: Yes
Handicapped Access: In the planning stage
Library/Research Facilities: Yes
By Subway: Nos. 1 or 9 to Franklin Street; No. 6, A, C, E, J, M, N, R or Z to Canal Street
By Bus: M6 or M10

31 · FRAUNCES TAVERN MUSEUM

Built in 1719 as a private residence, the structure was turned into a tavern in 1763 by Samuel Fraunces. Today the building, most of it dating from a restoration of 1907, and four adjacent nineteenth-century buildings house the museum, which offers changing and permanent exhibitions devoted to early American history and culture. The Visitor Orientation Exhibition presents an illustrated history of the tavern itself. The Long Room—the site of Washington's farewell to his officers after the Revolutionary War— has been restored as an eighteenth-century public-tavern room. Changing exhibits focus on a variety of topics.

Address/Telephone: 54 Pearl Street (at Broad Street), New York, NY 10004, (212) 425-1778

When to Visit: Mondays–Fridays—10 A.M. to 4:45 P.M. Saturdays—noon to 4 P.M.

Days/Holidays Closed: Sundays (*except* July 4 and December 4), New Year's Day, Thanksgiving and Christmas

Charges/Fees: Adults—$2.50; seniors, students—$1; children 6 and under—free

Suggested Grades: 3–adult

Guided Tour: By reservation; 30–45 minutes

Maximum Group: 45 adults; 35 students

Group Notice: Adults—1 month; students—4 months

Eating Facilities: None

Restroom Facilities: Yes

Handicapped Access: None

Gift Shop: Yes

Library/Research Facilities: None

By Subway: Nos. 4 or 5 to Bowling Green; Nos. 1 or 9 to South Ferry; N or R to Whitehall Street; J, M or Z to Broad Street

By Bus: M1, M6 or M15

32 · THE FRICK COLLECTION

The Frick Collection is housed in the former residence of Henry Clay Frick (1849–1919), one of the era's most powerful industrialists. Designed by Thomas Hastings, the building was constructed in 1913–14; after Mrs. Frick's death in 1931, changes and additions were made by architect John Russell Pope, and in 1935 the collection was opened to the public. It includes paintings by great European artists (Titian, Rembrandt, El Greco and Giovanni Bellini, among others), major works of sculpture (including one of the finest groups of small bronzes in the world), superb eighteenth-century French furniture and porcelains, Limoges enamels, Oriental rugs and works on paper. Special exhibitions are held during the year, along with lectures and concerts.

Address/Telephone: 1 East 70 Street (at Fifth Avenue), New York, NY 10021, (212) 288-0700

When to Visit: Tuesdays–Saturdays—10 A.M. to 6 P.M. Sundays, February 12, Election Day and November 11—1 P.M. to 6 P.M.

Days/Holidays Closed: Mondays, New Year's Day, July 4, Thanksgiving, Christmas Eve Day and Christmas

Charges/Fees: Adults—$5; seniors, students—$3

Suggested Grades: 6–adult (children under 10 are not admitted to the collection; those

under 16 must be accompanied by an adult)

Guided Tour: A special audiovisual program is presented hourly from 10:30 to 4:30 Tuesdays–Saturdays and from 1:30 to 4:30 Sundays

Group Notice: 4-week minimum

Eating Facilities: None

Restroom Facilities: Yes

Handicapped Access: Yes

Gift Shop: Yes

Library/Research Facilities: Yes (Frick Art Reference Library, at 10 East 71 Street, Mondays–Fridays—10 A.M. to 4:45 P.M.,

Saturdays—9:30 A.M. to 12:45 P.M. First-time visitors should arrive before 2:30 P.M., Mondays–Fridays, or before 11 A.M. on Saturdays for processing)

By Subway: No. 6 to 68 Street
By Bus: M1, M2, M3, M4, M18, M30, M66 or M72

General Grant National Memorial ("Grant's Tomb"). *National Park Service; photograph by Richard Frear)*

33 · GENERAL GRANT NATIONAL MEMORIAL

Popularly known as Grant's Tomb, the memorial to General Grant stands 150 feet high. Dedicated in 1897, the monument incorporates stylistic elements from the tomb of King Mausolus at Halicarnassus, the tomb of the Roman Emperor Hadrian in Rome and the Garfield Memorial in Cleveland. Designed by New York architect John Duncan, it features two recumbent figures by John Massey Rhind; the interior of the tomb is of Carrara and Lee marbles. Grant and his wife Julia lie in two sarcophagi in a rotunda, surrounded by mementos of Grant's life. The vaulting features allegorical reliefs, also designed by Rhind, representing Grant's birth, military life, political career and death.

Address/Telephone: Riverside Drive at West 122 Street, (212) 666-1640
Mailing Address: 26 Wall Street, New York, NY 10005
When to Visit: Daily—9 A.M. to 5 P.M.
Days/Holidays Closed: Christmas Day
Charges/Fees: Free
Suggested Grades: 4–adult
Guided Tour: Available upon request; 45 minutes

Maximum Group: 60
Group Notice: 2-week minimum
Eating Facilities: None
Restroom Facilities: None
Handicapped Access: None
Gift Shop: Yes
Library/Research Facilities: None
By Subway: Nos. 1 or 9 to West 116 Street
By Bus: M4, M5, M60 or M104

· GEORGE GUSTAV HEYE CENTER, SMITHSONIAN INSTITUTION: see NATIONAL MUSEUM OF THE AMERICAN INDIAN

· GUGGENHEIM MUSEUM [FIFTH & 88TH]: see SOLOMON R. GUGGENHEIM MUSEUM

34 · GUGGENHEIM MUSEUM SOHO

The Guggenheim Museum SoHo opened in 1992. It is located in a historic nineteenth-century building, with an interior designed for the museum by renowned architect Arata Isozaki. The exhibition site showcases traveling exhibitions and selections from the Guggenheim's permanent collection as well as special exhibitions that complement those at the Solomon R. Guggenheim Museum uptown.

Address/Telephone: 575 Broadway (at Prince Street), New York, NY 10012, (212) 423-3500

When to Visit: Sundays, Wednesdays, Thursdays and Fridays—11 A.M. to 6 P.M. Saturdays—11 A.M. to 8 P.M.

Days/Holidays Closed: Mondays and Tuesdays

Charges/Fees: Adults—$5; seniors, students—$3; members and children under 12—free

Suggested Grades: All grades

Guided Tour: By appointment only; 1 hour

Maximum Group: 50

Group Notice: 4–6 weeks (payment required in advance)

Eating Facilities: Yes (Café T)

Restroom Facilities: Yes

Handicapped Access: Yes

Gift Shop: Yes

Library/Research Facilities: None

By Subway: N or R to Prince Street; B, D, F or Q to Broadway–Lafayette Street; No. 6 to Spring Street

By Bus: M1, M5, M6 or M21

35 · GUINNESS WORLD OF RECORDS EXHIBITION

Located on the concourse level of the Empire State Building, the exhibitions bring the *Guinness Book of Records* to life. Visitors can view life-size models of the world's tallest man, smallest woman, heaviest man and oldest man, as well as entertainment stars such as Elvis Presley. Video screens throughout the exhibition allow visitors to witness Guinness records as they occurred; a cinema display presents milestones from such movies as *Ben-Hur* and *Batman*. Other exhibits include the "Animal Kingdom," which illustrates facts about all kinds of animals; an exhibit devoted to "The World of Sports"; and the "Hall of Fame"—a video presentation of Guinness' selection of six record-holders from among all those who have ever been inducted into the *Guinness Book of Records* Hall of Fame.

Address/Telephone: Concourse Level, Empire State Building, 350 Fifth Avenue (at West 34 Street), New York, NY 10118, (212) 947-2335

When to Visit: Mondays–Fridays—9 A.M. to 10 P.M. Saturdays and Sundays—9 A.M. to 10:30 P.M.

Charges/Fees: Adults—$6.95; seniors, students—$5.95; children—$3.50

Suggested Grades: 1–8

Guided Tour: Self-guided tours available; approximately 45 minutes

Maximum Group: 100

Group Notice: 2 weeks

Eating Facilities: None

Restroom Facilities: None

Handicapped Access: Yes

Gift Shop: Yes

Library/Research Facilities: None

By Subway: B, D, F, N, Q or R to 34 Street; No. 6 to 33 Street

By Bus: M1, M2, M3, M4, M5, M16, M18, M34 or Q32

inness World of Records.

36 · HISPANIC SOCIETY OF AMERICA

The society, founded in 1904, was established to provide a free public museum and research library representing the cultures of Hispanic peoples. The original collections, assembled by the founder, Archer Milton Huntington (1870–1955), as well as subsequent acquisitions, are housed in the main building located on Audubon Terrace. Holdings include unique examples of the fine and decorative arts of the Iberian Peninsula, dating from prehistory to the present, including works by Goya, Velázquez and El Greco. The library—an important center for research on Spanish and Portuguese art, history and literature—contains thousands of manuscripts and more than 200,000 early and modern books. The Iconography Collection contains prints, maps and globes, as well as an extensive photographic reference archive.

Address/Telephone: Audubon Terrace, Broadway and West 155 Street, New York, NY 10032, (212) 690-0743

Mailing Address: 613 West 155 Street, New York, NY 10032

When to Visit: Museum: Tuesdays–Saturdays—10 A.M. to 4:30 P.M. Sundays—1 P.M. to 4 P.M. Library Reading Room: Tuesdays–Fridays—1 P.M. to 4:15 P.M. Saturdays—10 A.M. to 4:15 P.M.

Days/Holidays Closed: Museum: Mondays, New Year's Day, February 12, February 22, Good Friday, Easter Sunday, May 30, July 4, Thanksgiving and Christmas. Library Reading Room: August, Easter weekend, Thanksgiving weekend, two weeks after the Saturday before Christmas and other days listed above

Charges/Fees: Free

Suggested Grades: 7–adult

Guided Tour: None. School groups by appointment only, call (212) 926-2234 for more information

Maximum Group: 50 (with 2 teachers)

Group Notice: Several weeks

Eating Facilities: None

Restroom Facilities: Yes

Handicapped Access: None

Gift Shop: Yes

Library/Research Facilities: Yes

By Subway: No. 1 or 9 to West 157 Street

By Bus: M4, M5 or Bx6

37 · INSTITUTE FOR CONTEMPORARY ART CLOCKTOWER GALLERY

The Institute for Contemporary Art, founded in 1971 as The Institute for Art and Urban Resources, Inc., was primarily dedicated to the transformation of abandoned and underutilized buildings in New York City into exhibition, performance and studio spaces for contemporary artists whose innovative work was often disregarded by the city's museum establishment. Today the institute operates two internationally acclaimed centers for contemporary art: the Clocktower Gallery and P.S. 1 Museum in Long

Island City (*see* Institute for Contemporary Art in the Queens section of this book). The Clocktower Gallery, established in 1972, is composed of a large main gallery and a tower exhibition space. The Institute's Education Program, which was founded in 1986, provides contemporary-art education, promoting public understanding and appreciation by allowing children and adults to interact with working artists.

Address/Telephone: 108 Leonard Street (between Broadway and Lafayette Street), New York, NY 10013, (212) 233-1096
When to Visit: Exhibition hours: Thursdays–Saturdays—noon to 6 P.M.
Days/Holidays Closed: Sundays–Wednesdays and all national holidays
Charges/Fees: Suggested donation—$2
Suggested Grades: 4–adult
Guided Tour: By appointment only (call Education Director for information)

Maximum Group: 40
Group Notice: 2-week minimum
Eating Facilities: None
Restroom Facilities: Yes
Handicapped Access: None
Gift Shop: None
Library/Research Facilities: None
By Subway: A, C, E, J, M, N, R, Z or No. 6 to Canal Street; Nos. 1 or 9 to Franklin Street
By Bus: M1 or M6

38 · INTERCHURCH CENTER

The Interchurch Center's wide variety of art exhibits changes ten times a year. The center itself contains many tributes to, and artistic celebrations of, ecumenical cooperation between Christian denominations.

Address/Telephone: 475 Riverside Drive (at West 120 Street), New York, NY 10115, (212) 870-2200
When to Visit: Mondays–Fridays—9 A.M. to 4:30 P.M.
Days/Holidays Closed: Saturdays, Sundays, New Year's Day, Martin Luther King, Jr.'s Birthday, Presidents' Day, Good Friday, Memorial Day, July 4, Labor Day, Columbus Day, Election Day, Thanksgiving Day, Christmas Eve Day and Christmas
Charges/Fees: Free
Suggested Grades: 1–adult

Guided Tour: Available on request; 30 to 60 minutes
Maximum Group: 50
Group Notice: 1 month
Eating Facilities: Yes (cafeteria). Picnic facilities available across the street at Grant's Tomb
Restroom Facilities: Yes
Handicapped Access: Yes
Gift Shop: Yes
Library/Research Facilities: Yes
By Subway: Nos. 1 or 9 to 116 Street
By Bus: M4, M5, M60 or M104

39 · INTERNATIONAL CENTER OF PHOTOGRAPHY

The International Center of Photography, New York City's only museum dedicated exclusively to the medium, was established in 1974 to collect, preserve and exhibit notable works, primarily from the twentieth century;

to teach photography at all levels; and to provide a critical forum for the exchange of ideas and information. Housed in an elegant town house of 1914, the center maintains a year-round schedule of exhibition and education programs and a permanent collection of some 30,000 images. Exhibition spaces are located at the headquarters building at 1130 Fifth Avenue (at East 94 Street) and the satellite galleries at 1133 Avenue of the Americas (at West 43 Street). Each facility houses a screening room and a museum shop.

International Center of Photography. *(Photograph by W. Hartshorn;* © *W. Hartshorn/ IPC)*

Address/Telephone: 1130 Fifth Avenue (at East 94 Street), New York, NY 10128, (212) 860-1777
When to Visit: Tuesdays—11 A.M. to 8 P.M. Wednesdays–Sundays—11 A.M. to 6 P.M.
Days/Holidays Closed: Mondays, New Year's Day, Thanksgiving and Christmas
Charges/Fees: General admission—$4; seniors, students—$2.50
Suggested Grades: All grades
Guided Tour: By appointment only; 1-1½ hours (special activities for school children)

Maximum Group: 40
Group Notice: 2 weeks
Eating Facilities: None
Restroom Facilities: Yes
Handicapped Access: Guards will assist with entry; elevator is accessible
Gift Shop: Yes
Library/Research Facilities: Yes
By Subway: Nos. 4 or 5 to 86 Street; No. 6 to 96 Street or to 86 Street
By Bus: M1, M2, M3, M4, M18 or M96

40 · INTERNATIONAL CENTER OF PHOTOGRAPHY—MIDTOWN

Address/Telephone: 1133 Avenue of the Americas (at West 43 Street), New York, NY 10036, (212) 768-4682
When to Visit: Tuesdays—11 A.M. to 8 P.M. Wednesdays–Sundays—11 A.M. to 6 P.M.
Days/Holidays Closed: Mondays, New Year's Day, Thanksgiving and Christmas
Charges/Fees: General admission—$4; seniors, students—$2.50
Suggested Grades: All grades
Guided Tour: By appointment only; 1-1½ hour (special activities for school children)

Maximum Group: 40
Group Notice: 2 weeks
Eating Facilities: None
Restroom Facilities: Yes
Handicapped Access: Yes
Gift Shop: Yes
Library/Research Facilities: By appointment only (archives and collections)
By Subway: B, D, F or Q to 42 Street; Nos. 1, 2, 3, 9, N or R to 42 Street–Times Square
By Bus: M1, M2, M3, M4, M5, M6, M7, M18, M42 or M104

41 · *INTREPID* SEA-AIR-SPACE MUSEUM

After 37 years of naval service, the U.S.S. *Intrepid,* a 40,000-ton, 900-foot-long aircraft carrier, was scheduled to be scrapped. It was saved in a campaign led by Zachary and Elizabeth Fisher and opened as a museum in August 1982; in 1985, it was designated a National Historic Landmark. The *Intrepid*'s major exhibition spaces are located in the hull and hangar deck, with other displays and artifacts on the pier and alongside, including the nuclear-missile submarine U.S.S. *Growler* and the destroyer U.S.S. *Edson.* The world's fastest aircraft, the Lockheed A-12 Blackbird reconnaissance jet, and the 1936 Coast Guard lightship *Nantucket* are also part of the museum's "fleet." The museum also offers the "Undersea Frontier," an exhibit with everything from live fish to recovered sunken treasures.

Address/Telephone: Pier 86, West 46 Street (at Twelfth Avenue), New York, NY 10036, (212) 245-2533

When to Visit: Memorial Day–Labor Day week: daily—10 A.M. to 5 P.M. (Last admission, 4 P.M.). Winter hours: Wednesdays–Sundays—10 A.M. to 5 P.M. (Last admission, 4 P.M.)

Charges/Fees: Adults—$7; seniors, veterans—$6; children under 12—$4; children under 6, uniformed armed forces members (with valid ID) and museum members—free

Suggested Grades: All grades

Guided Tour: None for U.S.S. Intrepid, though there is a guided tour for the U.S.S. Growler

Maximum Group: None

Group Notice: 24 hours

Eating Facilities: Yes (snack bar). Picnic facilities are available

Restroom Facilities: Yes

Handicapped Access: There is an elevator to the ship, but the flight deck is not accessible

Gift Shop: Yes

Library/Research Facilities: None

By Subway: A, C or E to 42 Street

By Bus: M16, M42 or M50

Additional Information: The M16 and M42 buses can be boarded at the 42 Street subway stop for those who might find the walk too long

42 · JAPAN SOCIETY GALLERY

Housed in a structure designed by Junzo Yoshimura and built in 1971, the Japan Society Gallery is one of the few museums in the United States dedicated solely to the exhibition of the arts of Japan—painting, sculpture, architecture and design, calligraphy, ceramics, woodblock prints, lacquerware and folk art. Bridging traditional and contemporary Japanese art and culture, the gallery explores Japanese aesthetics. Collaborating with renowned scholars, artists, museums and collectors worldwide, the gallery promotes global appreciation of Japanese culture. In addition to the gallery, the Japan Society (founded in 1907) includes a wide variety of educational symposia, lectures and business conferences in its activities through its U.S.–Japan Program. The Japan Society's Film Center is the preeminent showcase for Japanese cinema in the United States, and the society has introduced American audiences to traditional and modern Japanese performing arts through its special Performance Arts Program. The C. V. Starr Library houses a comprehensive collection of English-language books on Japanese history, culture, society, politics, arts, economics and religion.

Address/Telephone: 333 East 47 Street, New York, NY 10017, (212) 832-1155

When to Visit: Tuesdays–Sundays—11 A.M. to 5 P.M.

Days/Holidays Closed: Mondays and some holidays, depending on exhibition

Charges/Fees: Suggested donation—$3

Suggested Grades: All grades

Guided Tour: Yes; 1-hour maximum

Maximum Group: 25–30

Group Notice: 2–3 months. Call (212) 715-1253

Eating Facilities: None

Restroom Facilities: Yes

Handicapped Access: Yes

Gift Shop: (Exhibition catalogs and society publications only)

By Subway: No. 6 to 51 Street; E or F to Lexington Avenue

By Bus: M15, M27, M50, M101 or M102

43 · JEWISH MUSEUM

Founded in 1904, the museum operates under the auspices of the Jewish Theological Seminary of America. Located on New York City's "Museum Mile," it is housed in the landmark Warburg mansion, built in 1908 and donated to the seminary in 1947; the building was renovated and a new wing was built in 1993. Included within the 17 galleries devoted to the museum's permanent exhibition—"Culture and Continuity: The Jewish Journey"—are the recreation of an ancient synagogue, a two-story space featuring rare ceremonial art, a sculpture by George Segal that interprets the Holocaust, paintings and a video presentation on the contemporary Jewish experience. The museum also mounts special exhibitions and houses the Goodkind Resource Center, which offers extended viewings of selected television and radio programs from the museum's broadcast archive. The Edgar M. Bronfman Center for Education provides classroom spaces, a family center and a children's exhibition gallery.

Address/Telephone: 1109 Fifth Avenue (at East 92 Street), New York, NY 10128, (212) 423-3200 or (212) 423-3230

When to Visit: Sundays, Mondays, Wednesdays and Thursdays—11 A.M. to 5:45 P.M. Tuesdays—11 A.M. to 8 P.M.

Days/Holidays Closed: Fridays, Saturdays and all major federal and Jewish holidays

Charges/Fees: Adults—$7; seniors, students—$5; members, children under 12—free

Suggested Grades: All grades (children must be accompanied by an adult)

Guided Tour: Gallery tours available Mondays–Thursdays (noon and 2:30 P.M.) and Tuesdays (noon, 2:30 P.M. and 6 P.M.)

Maximum Group: 50

Group Notice: Call (212) 423-3225 for group-tour information

Eating Facilities: Yes (Café Weissman)

Restroom Facilities: Yes

Handicapped Access: Yes

Gift Shop: Yes

Library/Research Facilities: None

By Subway: Nos. 4, 5 or 6 to 86 Street; No. 6 to 96 Street

By Bus: M1, M2, M3, M4, M18 or M96

44 · LIBRARY AND MUSEUM FOR THE PERFORMING ARTS

The New York Public Library for the Performing Arts houses the world's most extensive combination of circulating, reference and rare archival collections devoted to the history of dance, theater, music and recorded sound. Research collections include the Music Division, Dance Collection, Rodgers & Hammerstein Archives of Recorded Sound and Billy Rose Theatre Collection. The circulating collection includes books on theater, dance, music, film and TV, music scores, audio recordings and video tapes, all of which can be borrowed by anyone with a library card. The library also sponsors a year-long exhibitions program, the Bruno Walter Auditorium series of free performances, the *Reading Room Readings* series of new plays and *Speaking Out,* a lecture series on issues relating to the performing arts.

Address/Telephone: 40 Lincoln Center Plaza (at West 65 Street), New York, NY 10023, (212) 870-1600
When to Visit: Exhibition hours: Mondays and Thursdays—noon to 8 P.M. Tuesdays, Wednesdays, Fridays and Saturdays—noon to 6 P.M.
Days/Holidays Closed: Sundays and all legal holidays

Charges/Fees: Free
Guided Tour: Wednesdays at 2 P.M.
Eating Facilities: None
Restroom Facilities: Yes
Handicapped Access: Yes
By Subway: Nos. 1 or 9 to 66 Street
By Bus: M5, M7, M10, M11, M66 or M104

45 · LOWER EAST SIDE TENEMENT MUSEUM

Chartered in 1988, the Lower East Side Tenement Museum presents exhibitions exploring the large variety of immigrant experiences on New York's Lower East Side. The museum features an 1863 tenement house— the first to be designated a National Historic Landmark—in which two recently restored apartments document the life of two immigrant families at different periods. The museum also offers dramatic performances, workshops and lectures, as well as Sunday walking tours through the Lower East Side. In addition, educational programs bring American immigrant history to students and organizations throughout the country.

Address/Telephone: 90 Orchard Street (at Broome Street), New York, NY 10002, (212) 431-0233
Mailing Address: 66 Allen Street, New York, NY 10002
When to Visit: Tuesdays–Fridays—11 A.M. to 5 P.M. Sundays—11 A.M. to 6 P.M. (Call for tenement-tour schedule)
Days/Holidays Closed: Mondays, Saturdays, New Year's Day, Thanksgiving and Christmas
Charges/Fees: Museum gallery: adults—$3; seniors—$2; students—$1 (on Tuesdays, gallery admission is free). Tenement tours (including gallery): adults—$7; seniors— $6; students—$5. Neighborhood walking tours (Sundays only): adults—$12; seniors, students—$10
Suggested Grades: 3–adult
Guided Tour: Tours of the 1863 tenement building last 45 minutes. Neighborhood walking tours (on Sundays) last 2 hours

Maximum Group: Public tours, 14; reserved groups, approximately 50 (negotiable)
Group Notice: 4-week minimum
Eating Facilities: None
Restroom Facilities: Yes
Handicapped Access: Limited
Gift Shop: Yes
Library/Research Facilities: None
By Subway: F to Delancey Street; J, M or Z to Essex Street; B, D or Q to Grand Street
By Bus: M9, M14, M15, M101 or M102
Additional Information: Four hours of free parking are available nearby on Broome Street, between Norfolk and Suffolk Streets. Call (212) 431-0233 for Sunday walking-tour topics. Sunday walking tours are at 12:30 and 2:30 P.M.

The building (indicated by the arrow) that currently houses the Lower East Side Tenement Museum, as it appeared in the 1930s. *(Municipal Archives, City of New York)*

• MERCHANT'S HOUSE MUSEUM: *see* OLD MERCHANT'S
  HOUSE

Metropolitan Museum of Art, Fifth Avenue facade. *(Metropolitan Museum of Art)*

46 • METROPOLITAN MUSEUM OF ART

Founded in 1870, the Metropolitan Museum is one of the world's largest,
its collections including more than two million works of art spanning 5000
years of world culture, from prehistory to the present. The American Wing
houses the world's most comprehensive collection of American paintings,
sculpture and decorative arts and includes 24 furnished period rooms. The
European paintings collection has more than 3000 works by such artists as
Rembrandt, Vermeer, Leonardo and Raphael, as well as Impressionist and

Post-Impressionist works, including canvases by Monet, Renoir and van Gogh. Other major collections include arms and armor, medieval and Renaissance art, Asian art, costumes, musical instruments, primitive art, drawings, prints, antiquities from around the ancient world (including the Egyptian Temple of Dendur), photography and twentieth-century art. More than 30 exhibitions are mounted each year. The museum also offers extensive education programs, including tours, lectures, symposia, film showings, teacher-training workshops, visitor information, reference library services and apprenticeship and fellowship programs.

Address/Telephone: 1000 Fifth Avenue (at 82 Street), New York, NY 10028, (212) 879-5500

When to Visit: Tuesdays–Thursdays and Sundays—9:30 A.M. to 5:15 P.M. Fridays and Saturdays—9:30 A.M. to 8:45 P.M.

Days/Holidays Closed: Mondays, New Year's Day, Thanksgiving and Christmas

Charges/Fees: Suggested donation (also covers visits to The Cloisters on the same day): adults—$7; seniors, students—$3.50; members, children under 12 with an adult—free

Suggested Grades: All grades

Guided Tour: Yes; 50 minutes to 1 hour

Maximum Group: 25–30

Group Notice: 3 weeks

Eating Facilities: Yes

Restroom Facilities: Yes

Handicapped Access: Yes

Gift Shop: Yes

Library/Research Facilities: Yes

By Subway: Nos. 4, 5 or 6 to 86 Street; No. 6 to 77 Street

By Bus: M1, M2, M3, M4, M18, M79 or M86

47 · MORRIS-JUMEL MANSION

The Morris-Jumel Mansion is the oldest private dwelling extant in Manhattan. Built in 1765 by British Colonel Roger Morris, the house was abandoned at the outbreak of the Revolutionary War and served as headquarters to George Washington in the autumn of 1776. Stephen and Eliza Jumel bought and remodeled the mansion in 1810 and, in 1833, after her husband's death, the imperious Madame Jumel married her second husband, Aaron Burr (then 77 years old). Listed in the National Register of Historic Places, the mansion now serves as a historic-house museum. The exterior is almost entirely original, an outstanding example of Colonial and Federal architecture. There are nine restored rooms in the mansion, two halls and a Colonial kitchen. The octagonal drawing room reflects the Morris period, with its hand-painted Chinese wallpaper and eighteenth-century British and American furniture; numerous pieces of original Jumel furniture are on display in the front parlor, in which Madame Jumel and Burr were married. There are special exhibition areas and a library and archival research space on the third floor.

Address/Telephone: 65 Jumel Terrace (at West 160 Street), New York, NY 10032, (212) 923-8008

When to Visit: Wednesdays–Sundays—10 A.M. to 4 P.M.

Days/Holidays Closed: Mondays, Tuesdays, New Year's Day, July 4, Thanksgiving and Christmas

Charges/Fees: Adults—$3; seniors, students—$2; children under 10 with an adult—free

Suggested Grades: 3–adult

Guided Tour: By appointment only; 1 hour

Maximum Group: 30

Group Notice: 2 weeks

Eating Facilities: None. Picnic facilities available

Restroom Facilities: Yes

Handicapped Access: None

Gift Shop: Yes

Library/Research Facilities: Open to Friends of Morris-Jumel Mansion only

By Subway: According to schedule, A, B or C to 163 Street; No. 1 to 157 Street

By Bus: M2, M3, M18, M100 or M101

48 · MUNICIPAL ART SOCIETY'S URBAN CENTER

Founded by a group of architects, mural painters, sculptors and civic leaders in 1893, the Municipal Art Society had as its original goal to beautify New York with public art. The society's mission has broadened to include protecting New York's architectural and cultural heritage. To facilitate this, the Urban Center was founded in 1980. Housed in the landmark Villard Houses (built in 1884 by McKim, Mead & White for publisher Henry Villard), it is the city's first center for cross-sector discussions of architecture, preservation and planning issues, providing information through public forums, seminars and publications. The Urban Center Galleries offer a variety of exhibitions pertaining to the city.

Address/Telephone: 457 Madison Avenue (at East 51 Street), New York, NY 10022, (212) 935-3960

When to Visit: Mondays–Wednesdays—11 A.M. to 5 P.M. Fridays and Saturdays—11 A.M. to 5 P.M.

Days/Holidays Closed: Thursdays, Sundays, New Year's Day, Labor Day, Memorial Day, Thanksgiving and Christmas

Charges/Fees: Free

Suggested Grades: All grades

Guided Tour: By appointment only (call for specific information)

Maximum Group: No maximum

Group Notice: 2 weeks

Eating Facilities: None

Restroom Facilities: Yes

Handicapped Access: Yes

Gift Shop: Yes, Urban Center Books, (212) 935-3595

Library/Research Facilities: Yes, The Greenacre Reference and Information Exchange

By Subway: E or F to Fifth Avenue; N or R to 49 Street; Nos. 1 or 9 to 50 Street; B, D, F or Q to 47–50 Streets–Rockefeller Center

By Bus: M1, M2, M3, M4 or M5

49 · MUSEO DEL BARRIO

Established in 1969, El Museo del Barrio houses a permanent collection of more than 8000 objects, including over 1000 pre-Columbian ceramics and vessels, 80 Mexican masks, over 300 *santos* (carved wooden figures made by artisans for devotional purposes) and over 6400 paintings, sculptures, works on paper and photographs by artists of Latin American descent.

Address/Telephone: 1230 Fifth Avenue (at East 104 Street), New York, NY 10029, (212) 831-7272

When to Visit: Wednesdays–Sundays—11 A.M. to 5 P.M.

Days/Holidays Closed: Mondays, Tuesdays and all legal holidays

Charges/Fees: Suggested donations: adults—$4; seniors, students (with IDs)—$2

Suggested Grades: All grades

Guided Tour: By appointment only; 30–45 minutes

Maximum Group: 30

Group Notice: 2 weeks

Eating Facilities: None. Picnic facilities available across the street in Central Park

Restroom Facilities: Yes

Handicapped Access: Yes

Gift Shop: Yes

Library/Research Facilities: By appointment only

By Subway: No. 6 to 103 Street

By Bus: M1, M2, M3, M4, M18 or M96

Additional Information: Phone lines announce current exhibitions; call for updated announcements

50 · MUSEUM AT THE FASHION INSTITUTE OF TECHNOLOGY

The museum attracts thousands of students, designers, researchers, fashion writers and historians who come to study its singular collection of apparel dating from the eighteenth century to the present, with a strong emphasis on twentieth-century costume. Its extraordinary textile collection includes 30,000 textiles dating from the eighteenth through the twentieth centuries, 250,000 indexed textile swatches and 1300 sample books from around the world. The museum's 13,000 square feet of space are used for exhibitions that explore broad issues of interior design, textiles, communications and advertising, marketing, photography, graphics and toy design.

Address/Telephone: Seventh Avenue at West 27 Street (between Seventh and Eighth Avenues), New York, NY 10001, (212) 760-7760

When to Visit: Exhibition hours: Tuesdays–Fridays—noon to 8 P.M. Saturdays—10 A.M. to 5 P.M. Call for exhibition schedule

Days/Holidays Closed: Sundays, Mondays and all legal holidays

Charges/Fees: Free

Suggested Grades: 9–adult

Guided Tour: Available for some exhibitions and for the Costume and Textile Collections

Maximum Group: 25 ($150 per group of 25)

Group Notice: 2 months

Eating Facilities: None

Restroom Facilities: Yes

Handicapped Access: Yes

Gift Shop: Campus bookstore

Library/Research Facilities: Yes (for design professionals with memberships)

By Subway: Nos. 1 or 9 to 28 Street; B, D, F, N, Q or R to 34 Street

By Bus: M5, M6, M7, M10 or M16

51 • MUSEUM FOR AFRICAN ART IN SOHO

This museum, located on the new "museum row" of lower Broadway in SoHo, is one of only two museums in the United States devoted exclusively to African art. Since it opened in 1984, the museum has organized many major exhibitions, beginning with its inaugural exhibition, "African Masterpieces from the Musée de l'Homme," which presented 100 objects from the Paris collection in which Picasso first discovered African art. Other programs offered by the museum include tours, storytelling, drumming, dance performances, lectures and films.

Address/Telephone: 593 Broadway (between Houston and Prince Streets), New York, NY 10012, (212) 966-1313
When to Visit: Tuesdays–Fridays—10:30 A.M. to 5:30 P.M. Saturdays and Sundays—noon to 6 P.M.
Days/Holidays Closed: Mondays, New Year's Day, Thanksgiving and Christmas
Charges/Fees: Adults—$4; seniors, children under 12—$2
Suggested Grades: All grades
Guided Tour: Tours available for children, with hands-on activities. 1-hour tours for adults available on Saturdays at 2 P.M.

Maximum Group: School groups, 40 students
Group Notice: School groups, 2 weeks; others should arrive at the museum shortly before 2 P.M. on Saturdays
Eating Facilities: None
Restroom Facilities: Yes
Handicapped Access: Yes
Gift Shop: Yes
Library/Research Facilities: None
By Subway: N or R to Prince Street; B, D, F or Q to Broadway–Lafayette Street; No. 6 to Spring Street
By Bus: M1, M5, M6 or M21

52 • MUSEUM OF AFRICAN AMERICAN HISTORY & ART

The Museum of African American History & Art houses the largest collection of black-oriented cinema within New York State. The collection has over 6000 titles, including rare and historic shorts and feature films dating back to 1909. Each September the museum sponsors a free seven-day conference on the importance of these films, featuring lectures by scholars and critics.

Address/Telephone: Second Floor Art Gallery, Adam Clayton Powell, Jr., State Office Building, 163 West 125 Street, New York, NY 10027, (212) 749-5298
When to Visit: Mondays–Fridays—11 A.M. to 3 P.M. (or by special appointment)

Days/Holidays Closed: All major observed holidays
Charges/Fees: Art gallery: free
Suggested Grades: 5–adult
Guided Tour: By appointment only
Maximum Group: Varies

Group Notice: 20–30 days
Eating Facilities: Yes (cafeteria on third floor)
Restroom Facilities: Yes
Handicapped Access: Yes
Gift Shop: None

Library/Research Facilities: Yes (scholars only)
By Subway: Nos. 2, 3, A, B (according to schedule), C or D to 125 Street
By Bus: M2, M7, M10, M60, M100, M101 or M102

53 · MUSEUM OF AMERICAN FINANCIAL HISTORY

Founded in 1988, the Museum of American Financial History collects and preserves historical financial artifacts. The museum is located in the heart of New York's financial district and presents specialized exhibits, each one covering a part of the history of America's capital markets.

Address/Telephone: 26 Broadway, New York, NY 10004, (212) 908-4110
When to Visit: Mondays–Fridays—11:30 A.M. to 2:30 P.M.
Days/Holidays Closed: Saturdays, Sundays, New Year's Day, Good Friday, Memorial Day, July 4, Labor Day, Thanksgiving and Christmas
Charges/Fees: Free
Suggested Grades: 5–adult

Guided Tour: None
Maximum Group: 20
Eating Facilities: None
Restroom Facilities: None
Handicapped Access: None
Gift Shop: Catalog sales
By Subway: Nos. 4 or 5 to Bowling Green; Nos. 1, 9, N or R to Rector Street
By Bus: M1, M6 or M15

54 · MUSEUM OF AMERICAN FOLK ART

Dazzling quilts, fancifully painted tinware and imaginatively carved folk sculpture are examples of American folk expressions from the museum's permanent collection. The Museum of American Folk Art, founded in 1961, is located on Manhattan's Upper West Side, directly opposite Lincoln Center. It is the leading urban institution dedicated to preserving the rich cultural history of the nation through exhibitions, educational programs and publications of the highest quality, including the award-winning magazine *Folk Art*.

Address/Telephone: 2 Lincoln Square (between West 65 and 66 Streets), New York, NY 10023, (212) 595-9533
Mailing Address: 61 West 62 Street, New York, NY 10023

When to Visit: Tuesdays–Sundays—11:30 A.M. to 7:30 P.M.
Days/Holidays Closed: Mondays, New Year's Day, July 4, Thanksgiving and Christmas
Charges/Fees: Free

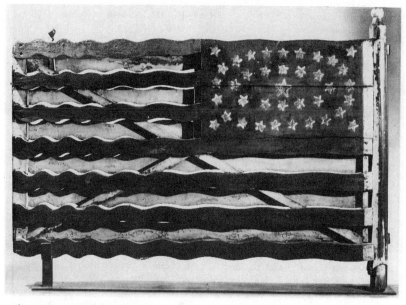

Flag gate, ca. 1876, in the collection of the Museum of American Folk Art. *(Photograph by Helga Photo Studio)*

Suggested Grades: All grades
Guided Tour: Yes; approximately 1 hour
Maximum Group: 30
Group Notice: 1 month
Eating Facilities: None
Restroom Facilities: Yes

Handicapped Access: Yes
Gift Shop: Yes. Second location at 62 West 50 Street, (212) 247-5611
Library/Research Facilities: Yes
By Subway: Nos. 1 or 9 to 66 Street
By Bus: M5, M7, M10, M11, M66 or M104

• MUSEUM OF AMERICAN ILLUSTRATION: *see* SOCIETY OF ILLUSTRATORS

55 • MUSEUM OF MODERN ART

Known throughout the world for its quality, scope and diversity, the museum's collection offers an unparalleled overview of the modern movement, including more than 100,000 paintings, sculptures, drawings, prints, photographs, architectural models and plans, and design objects. Artists represented include Picasso, Matisse, van Gogh, Pollock, de

Kooning, Rothko, Cézanne and Monet—to name but a few. The museum also owns some 10,000 films (with frequent viewings) and three million film stills, as well as 100,000 books and periodicals, all housed in the museum library.

Address/Telephone: 11 West 53 Street, New York, NY 10019, (212) 708-9480

When to Visit: Saturdays–Tuesdays—11 A.M. to 6 P.M. Thursdays and Fridays—noon to 8:30 P.M.

Days/Holidays Closed: Wednesdays, Thanksgiving and Christmas

Charges/Fees: Adults—$8; seniors (65+), students (with full-time student ID)—$5; members, children under 16 with an adult—free. Pay what you wish on Thursdays and Fridays, 5:30 P.M. to 8:30 P.M.

Suggested Grades: All grades

Guided Tour: Gallery talks (weekdays, except Wednesdays) Saturdays, Sundays and Mondays, 1 P.M. and 3 P.M.; Tuesdays, 1 P.M., 3 P.M. and 4 P.M.; Thursdays, 3 P.M., 6 P.M. and 7 P.M.; Fridays 3 P.M., 4 P.M., 6 P.M. and 7 P.M. Group tours by appointment only

Eating Facilities: Yes (Sette MoMA and The Garden Café). Picnic facilities in the Abby Aldrich Rockefeller Sculpture Garden

Restroom Facilities: Yes

Handicapped Access: Yes

Gift Shop: MoMA Book Store and MoMA Design Store (44 West 53 Street)

Library/Research Facilities: Call library reference desk, (212) 708-9433

By Subway: E or F to Fifth Avenue; N or R to 49 Street; Nos. 1 or 9 to 50 Street, B, D, F or Q to 47–50 Streets–Rockefeller Center

By Bus: M1, M2, M3, M4 or M5

Additional Information: MoMA also offers slide talks on Saturdays and Sundays at 1 P.M. and 2 P.M., and "Conversations with Contemporary Artists" Friday evenings at 6:30 P.M. Lecturers are available for tours of the museum and for slide lectures at outside locations. Call Special Programs for more information, (212) 708-9795. For information about MoMA's film screenings, call (212) 708-9857

56 · MUSEUM OF TELEVISION & RADIO

Founded by William S. Paley in 1975, the Museum of Television & Radio collects and preserves tapes of television and radio programs. The museum's collection includes more than 60,000 programs covering over 70 years of television and radio history, gathered from news, public-affairs programs, documentaries, performing arts, children's programming, sports, comedy and advertising. The museum draws from its collection to present exhibitions, screenings and listening series that focus on topics of social, historical, popular or artistic interest. Visitors can use the museum's library catalog system to choose specific programs and privately watch or listen to selections. Seminars and an extensive education program are offered as well.

Address/Telephone: 25 West 52 Street (between Fifth and Sixth Avenues), New York, NY 10019, (212) 621-6800

When to Visit: Tuesdays, Wednesdays, Saturdays and Sundays—noon to 6 P.M. Thursdays—noon to 8 P.M. Fridays—noon to 9 P.M. (theaters only)

Days/Holidays Closed: Mondays, New Year's Day, July 4, Thanksgiving and Christmas

Charges/Fees: Suggested donations: adults—$6; seniors, students—$4; children under 13—$3

Suggested Grades: All grades. Call the Education Department for information (212) 621-6600

Guided Tour: Yes (inquire at front desk for information)

Group Notice: Call Group Visits office from 3 P.M. to 5 P.M., Tuesdays–Fridays, (212) 621-6600

Maximum Group: Tours available for groups of 10 to 40. Call Group Visits office from 3 P.M. to 5 P.M., Tuesdays to Fridays, (212) 621-6600

Eating Facilities: None

Restroom Facilities: Yes

Handicapped Access: Yes

Gift Shop: Yes

Library/Research Facilities: Yes

By Subway: E or F to Fifth Avenue; N or R to 49 Street; Nos. 1 or 9 to 50 Street; B, D, F or Q to 47–50 Streets–Rockefeller Center

By Bus: M1, M2, M3, M4, M5, M6, M7, M18, M27, M50 or M57

Museum of Television & Radio. *(Photograph by Norman McGrath)*

57 · MUSEUM OF THE CITY OF NEW YORK

From 1923 to 1932, the Museum of the City of New York was housed in historic Gracie Mansion, today the official residence of the Mayor of New York. Because of the increased number of its holdings, the museum was relocated to the present structure, built for it at Fifth Avenue, where it now maintains outstanding collections of portraits, prints, historical documents, decorative arts, toys, dolls and dollhouses, costumes, theatrical ephemera, photographs and sports memorabilia that document the city's history. The museum offers a wide variety of special programs, including school programs, teacher workshops, walking tours, lectures and concerts.

Address/Telephone: Fifth Avenue at East 103 Street, New York, NY 10029, (212) 534-1672

When to Visit: Wednesdays–Saturdays—10 A.M. to 5 P.M. Sundays—1 P.M. to 5 P.M. Tuesdays (for preregistered school and group tours)—10 A.M. to 2 P.M.

Days/Holidays Closed: Mondays, Tuesdays (except for preregistered school and group tours) and all legal holidays

Charges/Fees: Suggested donations: adults— $5; seniors, students, children—$3; families— $8

Suggested Grades: All grades. Call the Education Department for information, (212) 534-1672, ext. 206

Guided Tour: 1-hour guided tours available for adults and college groups on weekday afternoons and weekends by special arrangements

Maximum Group: 25–30

Group Notice: 4 weeks

Eating Facilities: None. Picnic facilities available in Central Park Conservatory Garden nearby

Restroom Facilities: Yes

Handicapped Access: Ramp access at East 104 Street entrance

Gift Shop: Yes

Library/Research Facilities: By appointment only

By Subway: No. 6 to 103 Street

By Bus: M1, M2, M3, M4 or M18

58 · NATIONAL ACADEMY OF DESIGN

The School of Fine Arts at the National Academy of Design is the oldest art school in New York, and its museum is home to an extraordinary collection of American art. Housed in a turn-of-the-century landmark building on Manhattan's "Museum Mile," the museum features one of the world's foremost collections of nineteenth- and twentieth-century American art, with nearly 8000 paintings, sculptures and works on paper. Among the leading artists and architects in the collection are Mary Cassatt, Richard Diebenkorn, Thomas Eakins, Winslow Homer, I. M. Pei, Robert Rauschenberg, John Singer Sargent and Frank Lloyd Wright. Lectures, symposia, artist's talks, tours and education programs are offered in conjunction with the collection and special exhibits.

Main staircase in rotunda, National Academy of Design.

Address/Telephone: 1083 Fifth Avenue (at East 89 Street), New York, NY 10128, (212) 369-4880

When to Visit: Wednesdays, Thursdays, Saturdays and Sundays—noon to 5 P.M. Fridays—noon to 8 P.M.

Days/Holidays Closed: Mondays, Tuesdays and all major holidays

Charges/Fees: General—$3.50; seniors, students, children under 16—$2; Academy Friends—free

Suggested Grades: All grades

Guided Tour: Yes; 45 minutes (available on the first and third Friday of every month at 6 P.M.)

Maximum Group: Students, 30; adults, 50 (accompanied by 2 docents)

Group Notice: 2-week minimum

Eating Facilities: None. Picnic facilities available in Central Park

Restroom Facilities: Yes

Handicapped Access: Yes

Gift Shop: Yes (books and postcards)

Library/Research Facilities: None

By Subway: Nos. 4, 5 or 6 to 86 Street

By Bus: M1, M2, M3, M4, M18, M86 or M96

59 • NATIONAL MUSEUM OF THE AMERICAN INDIAN GEORGE GUSTAV HEYE CENTER, SMITHSONIAN INSTITUTION

The National Museum of the American Indian at the George Gustav Heye Center, Smithsonian Institution—established by an Act of Congress in 1989—opened in October 1994 with three inaugural exhibitions mounted in the museum's new location, the Alexander Hamilton U.S. Custom House. Permanently housed in this magnificent Beaux-Arts structure, the collection is the finest and most comprehensive in the world. It includes more than one million objects, including 517,533 archaeological objects and 151,583 ethnological objects from almost every state in the United States, Canada, Mexico, Central and South America, the Caribbean and Greenland.

Address/Telephone: 1 Bowling Green (tip of Battery Park), New York, NY 10004, (212) 668-6624

When to Visit: Daily—10 A.M. to 5 P.M.

Days/Holidays Closed: Christmas

Charges/Fees: Free

Suggested Grades: All grades

Guided Tour: Reserved school group tours

Maximum Group: Depends on tour

Group Notice: As far in advance as possible

Eating Facilities: None. Picnic facilities available in Battery Park, next to the museum

Restroom Facilities: Yes

Handicapped Access: Yes

Gift Shop: Adults' and children's gift shops

Library/Research Facilities: Yes

By Subway: Nos. 4 or 5 to Bowling Green; Nos. 1 or 9 to South Ferry; N or R to Whitehall Street

By Bus: M1, M6 or M15

60 • NEW MUSEUM OF CONTEMPORARY ART

Devoted exclusively to contemporary art, the New Museum of Contemporary Art focuses primarily on living artists' works of the past ten years. Unlike traditional museums, there are no permanent displays; instead the museum presents three to four major exhibitions each year and three times as many smaller exhibitions. Since its founding in 1977, the museum has been a forum for artists grappling with contemporary issues and events, and prides itself on showing controversial, provocative, unknown or underrecognized works. The museum also offers innovative education programs.

Address/Telephone: 583 Broadway (between Houston and Prince Streets), New York, NY 10012, (212) 219-1355

When to Visit: Wednesdays–Fridays and Sundays—noon to 6 P.M. Saturdays—noon to 8 P.M.

Days/Holidays Closed: Mondays and Tuesdays

Charges/Fees: General—$4; seniors, students, artists—$3. Saturdays from 6 P.M. to 8 P.M.—free

Suggested Grades: All grades

Guided Tour: Yes; 40 minutes

Maximum Group: 30

Group Notice: 6 weeks

Eating Facilities: None

Restroom Facilities: Yes

Handicapped Access: Partial

Gift Shop: Yes

Library/Research Facilities: None

By Subway: No. 6 to Spring Street or to Bleecker Street; N or R to Prince Street; C or E to Spring Street; B, D, F or Q to Broadway–Lafayette Street

By Bus: M1, M5, M6 or M21

61 • NEW YORK CITY FIRE MUSEUM

The New York City Fire Museum, opened in 1987, is housed in a renovated 1904 firehouse located in Manhattan's SoHo area. It displays the most comprehensive collection of fire-related art and artifacts in the United States, from the mid-eighteenth century to the present. The collection includes beautifully preserved horse- and hand-drawn pieces of fire-fighting apparatus, fire buckets, trumpets, toy and working models, helmets, parade hats, portraits, photographs, Currier & Ives and other prints, and an important collection of fire-insurance marks. The museum is committed to bring fire-safety awareness to the public through its Fire Safety Education program, and it offers a fire-safety orientation lecture, two videotapes on fire prevention and an interpretive tour of the museum's

B.DALTON #1142

GREENWICH VILLAGE, NYC (212)674-8780

REG#02   BOOKSELLER#097
RECEIPT#   32023 05/17/96   10:34 PM

5 0486286398   NEW YORK CITY MUSEUM GDE
                       1 @ 3.95   3.95

SUBTOTAL   3.95
SALES TAX - 8.25%   .33
TOTAL   4.28
CASH PAYMENT   10.30
CHANGE   6.02

THANK YOU FOR SHOPPING AT B.DALTON!

own collection. The museum also plays a leading role in the research and study of the historical development of international, national and New York City fire fighting.

Address/Telephone: 278 Spring Street (between Varick and Hudson Streets), New York, NY 10013, (212) 691-1303

When to Visit: Tuesdays–Sundays—10 A.M. to 4 P.M. Thursdays (June–August)—10 A.M. to 9 P.M.

Days/Holidays Closed: Mondays, New Year's Day, July 4, Thanksgiving and Christmas

Charges/Fees: Suggested donations: adults— $3; children—50¢

Suggested Grades: All grades (tour adjusted to attention span and level of group)

Guided Tour: By appointment only

Maximum Group: 35

Group Notice: 2–3 months

Eating Facilities: None

Restroom Facilities: Yes

Handicapped Access: Yes

Gift Shop: Yes

Library/Research Facilities: By appointment only

By Subway: Nos. 1 or 9 to Houston Street; C or E to Spring Street

By Bus: M6, M10 or M21

La France horse-drawn pump steamer, 1901, New York City Fire Museum.

62 • NEW-YORK HISTORICAL SOCIETY

One of the first cultural and educational institutions established in the United States, the New-York Historical Society was founded in 1804. Over the years the society amassed huge and diverse holdings, and today its collections include such objects as George Washington's inaugural carriage and chair, John James Audubon's original watercolors for his *Birds of America*, paintings and drawings of the most distinguished Hudson River School artists, the nation's largest collection of Tiffany lamps, rare New York silver, eighteenth-century toys, the original model of the Civil War ironclad ship *Monitor*, the correspondence between Aaron Burr and Alexander Hamilton leading to their duel in 1804 and one of the country's largest collections of slavery and abolition materials. The society's research library is no less distinguished, consisting of eight miles of shelf space filled with over 650,000 books, two million manuscripts, 35,000 maps and atlases, 15,000 pieces of sheet music and 40,000 broadsides; significant collections include early trial literature, three centuries of restaurant menus, and naval and military materials relating to the Revolutionary War, the War of 1812, the Civil War and the Spanish-American War.

Address/Telephone: 2 West 77 Street (at Central Park West), New York, NY 10024, (212) 873-3400

When to Visit: Wednesday–Sunday—noon to 5 P.M.

Days/Holidays Closed: Sundays, Mondays, Tuesdays and all legal holidays.

Charges/Fees: Adults—$3; seniors, children—$1

Suggested Grades: 4–adult

Guided Tour: Yes; 45 minutes

Maximum Group: 25

Group Notice: 2 months

Eating Facilities: None

Restroom Facilities: Yes

Handicapped Access: Yes

Gift Shop: Yes

Library/Research Facilities: Yes

By Subway: B (according to schedule) or C to 81 Street; Nos. 1 or 9 to 79 Street

By Bus: M7, M10, M11, M72 or M79

63 • NEW YORK PUBLIC LIBRARY

In 1895, the private libraries of John Jacob Astor and James Lenox were consolidated through a trust left by Samuel J. Tilden, whose wish was to found a free public library. The City of New York agreed to erect and maintain the Central Research Library (now the Center for the Humanities) at Fifth Avenue and West 42 Street (designed by John Merven Carrère and Thomas Hastings). After ten years of construction, the building opened to the public on May 23, 1911. Today many visitors come to the library merely to see the impressive interior, including Astor Hall, where information desks provide floor plans and where the guided tours begin. Among the tour's highlights are the De Witt Wallace Periodical Room and the Edna B. Salomon Room, in which the library's art collection, including paintings by Gilbert Stuart and Sir Joshua Reynolds, are displayed, and, in addition to many specialized collections, the Main Reading Room, where scholars can consult (but cannot check out) selections from the library's more than 12 million books and 27 million other items. Each year the library mounts changing exhibitions as well as the ongoing exhibition "Building The New York Public Library," located on the second floor. Here reproductions of archival drawings, photographs, manuscripts and memorabilia illustrate the history and evolution of the library, and the planning, construction and decoration of the Beaux-Arts structure.

Address/Telephone: Fifth Avenue (at West 42 Street), New York, NY 10018, (212) 661-7220

When to Visit: Exhibition hours: Mondays, Thursdays–Saturdays—10 A.M. to 6 P.M. Tuesdays and Wednesdays—11 A.M. to 6 P.M.

Days/Holidays Closed: Sundays, Mondays (Berg Exhibition Room) and all legal holidays

Charges/Fees: Free

Guided Tour: Yes

Eating Facilities: None. Picnic facilities available in Bryant Park behind the library

Restroom Facilities: Yes

Handicapped Access: Yes

Gift Shop: Yes

By Subway: No. 7 to Fifth Avenue; B, D, F or Q to 42 Street; Nos. 1, 2, 3, 9, N or R to Times Square; Nos. 4, 5 or 6 to 42 Street–Grand Central

By Bus: M1, M2, M3, M5, M6, M7, M18, M42, M104 or Q32

Additional Information: Call (212) 661-7220 for hours of the various collections and reading rooms

• NEW YORK PUBLIC LIBRARY FOR THE PERFORMING ARTS: *see* LIBRARY AND MUSEUM FOR THE PERFORMING ARTS

64 • NEW YORK STOCK EXCHANGE VISITORS CENTER

The center offers the opportunity to view the NYSE trading floor, where 2600 companies list more than 145 billion shares of stock, valued at $4.6 trillion. Taped explanations of the activity are available in English, German, French, Italian, Japanese and Spanish. The center also features exhibits explaining the hows and whys of the NYSE market system, including how stocks are bought and sold. A film explains the market system, and interactive computer displays provide information on companies listed on the exchange and on how to retrieve financial information on stocks, bonds, futures or options. A live demonstration shows visitors how to read electronic ticker tape.

Address/Telephone: 20 Broad Street (near Wall Street), New York, NY 10005, (212) 656-5166

When to Visit: Mondays–Fridays—9:15 A.M. to 4 P.M.

Days/Holidays Closed: Weekends, New Year's Day, Washington's Birthday, Good Friday, Memorial Day, July 4, Labor Day, Thanksgiving and Christmas

Charges/Fees: Free

Suggested Grades: 7–adult

Guided Tour: None

Maximum Group: Scheduled groups, 25. Call (212) 656-5168 for more information

Group Notice: Several months

Eating Facilities: None

Restroom Facilities: Yes

Handicapped Access: Yes

Gift Shop: Yes

Library/Research Facilities: None

By Subway: Nos. 2, 3, 4 or 5 to Wall Street; Nos. 1, 9, N or R to Rector Street; J, M or Z to Broad Street

By Bus: M1, M6 or M15

65 · NEW YORK UNEARTHED: CITY ARCHAEOLOGY

A program of the South Street Seaport Museum, New York Unearthed is the only museum dedicated to New York's archaeological heritage. Here the remains of the past tell the story of New York's history as visitors explore exhibits of artifacts excavated from beneath city streets. The museum features special dioramas and a three-dimensional cross-section of an archaeological site. Visitors can also view archaeologists and conservators at work in a glass-enclosed state-of-the-art laboratory. The Unearthing New York Systems Elevator provides a simulated ride from the streets of Wall Street to the depths of an archaeological dig.

Address/Telephone: 17 State Street at Battery Park (between Pearl and Whitehall Streets), New York, NY 10004, (212) 748-8628

When to Visit: Mid-December–March: Mondays–Fridays—noon to 6 P.M. April–mid-December: Mondays–Saturdays—noon to 6 P.M.

Days/Holidays Closed: Saturdays (from mid-December–March), Sundays and major holidays

Charges/Fees: Free

Suggested Grades: 3–adult

Guided Tour: By appointment only; 1½ hours. Educational programs, tours and workshops for schoolchildren, special-needs groups and adults are also available. Call Group Tours at South Street Seaport Museum, (212) 748-8590

Maximum Group: 30

Group Notice: 2 months

Eating Facilities: None. Limited picnic facilities in courtyard

Restroom Facilities: Yes

Handicapped Access: Yes

Gift Shop: Yes

Library/Research Facilities: Yes

By Subway: Nos. 1 or 9 to South Ferry; Nos. 4 or 5 to Bowling Green; N or R to Whitehall Street

By Bus: M1, M6 or M15

66 · NICHOLAS ROERICH MUSEUM

Named for Russian-born artist, philosopher, scientist and humanitarian Nicholas Roerich (1874–1947), the museum maintains a permanent collection of Roerich paintings and published works. Roerich created over 6000 easel paintings, besides frescoes in churches and public buildings and designs for mosaics and architectural motifs. He painted décors for Diaghilev's Ballets Russes and for operas by Wagner, Moussorgsky, Borodin and Rimsky-Korsakov. Perhaps his greatest humanitarian achievement was the Roerich Pact and Banner of Peace (1935), providing for the international protection, in war and peace, of monuments and cultural institutions. In addition to exhibitions, the museum regularly schedules poetry readings and recitals by concert artists and chamber-music ensembles; and displays handicrafts by native and foreign artisans.

Address/Telephone: 319 West 107 Street (near Riverside Drive), New York, NY 10025, (212) 864-7752
When to Visit: Tuesdays–Sundays—2 P.M. to 5 P.M.
Days/Holidays Closed: Mondays and all major holidays (call for more information)
Charges/Fees: Free (donations accepted)
Suggested Grades: All grades (under supervision)
Guided Tour: None, though staff is available to answer questions

Maximum Group: 25
Group Notice: 1 week
Eating Facilities: None
Restroom Facilities: Yes
Handicapped Access: None
Gift Shop: Postcards, prints and books only
Library/Research Facilities: None
By Subway: Nos. 1 or 9 to Cathedral Parkway (110 Street)
By Bus: M4, M5, M104 or M116

67 · OLD MERCHANT'S HOUSE MUSEUM

The Merchant's House Museum is New York City's only family home preserved intact and unaltered from the nineteenth century, and Greenwich Village's only historic-house museum. Located just a few blocks from Washington Square, it was built in 1832 as a row house and was home to the merchant Seabury Tredwell and to his family from 1835 to 1933, when Gertrude Tredwell died there. Today the Merchant's House Museum is a designated National Historic and New York City Landmark, its late-Federal exterior standing out from the more modern architecture that surrounds it. The house's interior, reflecting changing tastes and fashions, contains original furniture, clothing and family memorabilia, and offers an intimate glimpse of upper-middle-class life in nineteenth-century New York. In addition to its wonderful and unique collection, the Merchant's House Museum also hosts a variety of events including concerts, plays, readings and lectures.

Old Merchant's House Museum.

Address/Telephone: 29 East 4 Street (between Lafayette Street and Bowery), New York, NY 10003, (212) 777-1089

When to Visit: Sundays–Thursdays—1 P.M. to 4 P.M.

Days/Holidays Closed: Fridays, Saturdays and all major holidays

Charges/Fees: Adults—$3; seniors, students (with ID)—$2; members, children under 12 with an adult—free

Suggested Grades: 3–adult (specially designed programs available for children, grades 3–6)

Guided Tour: Yes; 45 minutes to 1 hour (docent-guided tours offered on Sundays; printed information for self-guided tours available weekdays)

Maximum Group: 20

Group Notice: 1-week minimum (more advance notice preferred)

Eating Facilities: None

Restroom Facilities: Yes

Handicapped Access: None

Gift Shop: Yes

Library/Research Facilities: Yes

By Subway: No. 6 to Astor Place or to Bleecker Street; B, D, F or Q to Broadway–Lafayette Street; N or R to 8 Street

By Bus: M1, M5, M6, M8, M21, M101 or M102

68 · PAINE WEBBER ART GALLERY

Paine Webber sponsors four to five exhibitions a year, organized by New York–area nonprofit cultural institutions and mounted in the Paine Webber Art Gallery. Past exhibitions—held in conjunction with such organizations as the American Museum of the Moving Image, the Americas Society, the Museum of American Folk Art and the New-York Historical Society—have featured children's art, Mayan weavings, carousel horses, landscape design, contemporary folk art and photography.

Address/Telephone: 1285 Avenue of the Americas (between West 51 and 52 Streets), New York, NY 10019, (212) 713-2885
When to Visit: Mondays–Fridays—8 A.M. to 6 P.M.
Days/Holidays Closed: Saturdays and Sundays
Charges/Fees: Free
Suggested Grades: Depends on exhibition
Guided Tour: None
Maximum Group: 40
Group Notice: 1 week

Eating Facilities: Yes (cafeteria on second floor)
Restroom Facilities: Yes
Handicapped Access: Yes
Gift Shop: None
Library/Research Facilities: None
By Subway: B, D, F or Q to 47–50 Streets–Rockefeller Center; Nos. 1 or 9 to 50 Street; N or R to 49 Street
By Bus: M5, M6, M7, M27 or M50

69 · PIERPONT MORGAN LIBRARY

Housed in a turn-of-the-century Renaissance-style palazzo, the Pierpont Morgan Library is both a museum and a center for scholarly research. Its collection of rare books, manuscripts and drawings deals primarily with the history, art and literature of Western civilization from the Middle Ages to the twentieth century. The library presents a continuing program of exhibitions drawn from its own permanent collections, which originated with the medieval and Renaissance manuscripts, rare books and fine bindings, autograph manuscripts and master drawings collected by J. Pierpont Morgan (1837–1913). To complement the exhibitions, the library offers guided tours of both major exhibitions and the library's period West and East Rooms, along with video presentations, lectures and concerts.

Address/Telephone: 29 East 36 Street (between Madison and Fifth Avenues), New York, NY 10016, (212) 685-0008
When to Visit: Tuesdays–Fridays—10:30 A.M. to 5 P.M. Saturdays—10:30 A.M. to 6 P.M. Sundays—noon to 6 P.M.
Charges/Fees: Suggested donations: adults—$5; seniors, students—$3
Suggested Grades: 4–adult
Guided Tour: Yes; 45 minutes to 1 hour
Maximum Group: 40

Group Notice: 6 weeks
Eating Facilities: Yes (restaurant)
Restroom Facilities: Yes
Handicapped Access: Yes
Gift Shop: Yes
Library/Research Facilities: Yes
By Subway: No. 6 to 33 Street; Nos. 4, 5 or 7 to 42 Street–Grand Central; B, D, F, N, Q or R to 34 Street
By Bus: M1, M2, M3, M4, M5, M16, M18 or M34

70 · ROCKEFELLER CENTER

Comprised of 19 buildings on 22 acres in midtown Manhattan, Rockefeller Center was founded by John D. Rockefeller, Jr. The center originally consisted of 14 buildings constructed from 1931 to 1940; today it is the world's largest privately owned business and entertainment complex. Named a New York City landmark in 1985 and a National Historic Landmark in 1987, the center is home to many of the world's leading businesses, as shown by the names of many of its buildings, including The Associated Press, McGraw-Hill, Simon & Schuster, Time & Life, Time Warner and G.E. Buildings. The center is also home to the landmark Radio City Music Hall, which opened in 1932. Self-guided walking tours of the center (brochure available at the information desk in the G.E. Building, home to NBC Studios) allow visitors to view the center's buildings, gardens, parks and plazas. Among the highlights are more than 100 works of art by 30 of this century's foremost artists—brought to the center as part of its art program. Works include Lee Lawrie's *Wisdom,* executed in limestone and cast in glass, located above the main entrance of the G.E. Building, and Paul Manship's bronze and gold-leaf statue of *Prometheus,* located in the Lower Plaza. The Lower Plaza itself is home to the famous Rockefeller Center Skating Rink, open to the public in fall and winter; during spring and summer months it is home to the Summergarden restaurant. And, of course, during the winter holidays, "the most beautiful tree in the world" is lighted and stands as a well-known symbol of the holiday season.

Address/Telephone: 1230 Avenue of the Americas, New York, NY 10020, (212) 632-3975

Charges/Fees: Free

Suggested Grades: All grades

Guided Tour: Brochures for self-guided tours available at the information desk in the G.E. Building lobby, 365 days a year, from 8 A.M. to 6 P.M.

Eating Facilities: Yes

Restroom Facilities: Yes

Handicapped Access: Yes

Library/Research Facilities: None

By Subway: B, D, F or Q to 47–50 Streets–Rockefeller Center

By Bus: M1, M2, M3, M4, M5, M6, M7, M18, M27 or M50

71 · ROSE MUSEUM AT CARNEGIE HALL

Built in 1891 by William B. Tuthill, Carnegie Hall is one of the world's greatest concert halls. For 70 years it was home to the New York Philharmonic, and the world's most famous conductors, artists and musicians have appeared here—beginning on opening night, when Peter Ilyich Tchaikovsky conducted. Dvořák's New World Symphony had its world premiere in the hall. When the Philharmonic moved to Lincoln Center in 1962, Carnegie Hall's future was uncertain. Fortunately, it was saved by a group of concerned musicians and patrons, led by violinist Isaac Stern. The Rose Museum, housed on the second floor of Carnegie Hall, is devoted to the hall's history. It is divided into four sections: the history of the building itself, the history of the events on stage, the tenants of the studio tower, and the smaller halls. From time to time, temporary exhibits are arranged to coincide with an anniversary or special event on stage.

Address/Telephone: Second floor, 154 West 57 Street (at Seventh Avenue), New York, NY 10019, (212) 903-9629

Mailing Address: 881 Seventh Avenue, New York, NY 10019

When to Visit: Mondays, Tuesdays, Thursdays–Sundays—11 A.M. to 4:30 P.M. Open in the evenings for concert patrons

Days/Holidays Closed: August and Wednesdays

Charges/Fees: Free

Guided Tour: The regular tour of Carnegie Hall ends in the Rose Museum, but visitors are not required to take the tour in order to visit the museum

Eating Facilities: None

Restroom Facilities: Yes

Handicapped Access: Yes

Gift Shop: Yes

Library/Research Facilities: The Carnegie Hall Archives

By Subway: N or R to 57 Street; B (according to schedule) or Q to 57 Street; B (according to schedule), D or E to Seventh Avenue

By Bus: M6, M7, M10, M31, M57 or M104

Additional Information: For information about tours of Carnegie Hall (separate from the Rose Museum), call (212) 903-9790. For information on museum events and exhibitions, call the Carnegie Hall Archives, (212) 903-9629.

72 · SCHOMBURG CENTER FOR RESEARCH IN BLACK CULTURE

This branch of the New York Public Library system houses the country's largest library of black and African cultures, donated in 1926 by the distinguished black scholar and bibliophile Arthur A. Schomburg (1874–1938). Schomburg's collection included over 5000 volumes, 3000 manuscripts, 2000 etchings and paintings and several thousand pamphlets. Today the center's collections contain over 5 million items, including 300,000 images in the Photographs and Prints collection and an extensive Moving Image and Recorded Sound collection, which encompasses musical documentation, oral-history recordings, motion pictures and videotapes. The center also houses a Manuscripts, Archives and Rare Books collection and a comprehensive Art and Artifacts collection with over 10,000 paintings, sculptures, textiles and other artifacts. The research center exhibits works drawn from its own collections and resources from other institutions. It also sponsors a year-round schedule of events and activities that interpret and complement its resources, including seminars, forums, film screenings, performing-arts presentations and educational programming for children and adults.

Address/Telephone: 515 Malcolm X Boulevard (Lenox Avenue; at West 135 Street), New York, NY 10037, (212) 491-2200

When to Visit: Exhibition hours: Mondays–Wednesdays—noon to 8 P.M. Thursdays–Saturdays—10 A.M. to 6 P.M. Sundays—1 P.M. to 5 P.M.

Days/Holidays Closed: All legal holidays

Charges/Fees: Free

Suggested Grades: All grades

Guided Tour: By appointment only—Tuesdays and Wednesdays—10 A.M. to noon

Maximum Group: Call (212) 491-2200 for information

Eating Facilities: None

Restroom Facilities: Yes

Handicapped Access: Yes

Gift Shop: Yes

Library/Research Facilities: Yes

By Subway: Nos. 2 or 3 to 135 Street

By Bus: M1, M2, M7, M102 or Bx33

73 · SOCIETY OF ILLUSTRATORS MUSEUM OF AMERICAN ILLUSTRATION

Founded in 1901, the Society of Illustrators is housed in an 1875 carriage house. Here it operates two museum galleries that feature exhibitions on historic and contemporary themes, showing the art created for publication by such famous illustrators as Norman Rockwell, N. C. Wyeth, Charles Dana Gibson and James Montgomery Flagg. Magazines such as *National Geographic, Reader's Digest* and *Time* are often featured, as are paperback books, postal issues, humor, theater and film posters. Displayed throughout the building are items selected from the society's permanent collection of over 2000 works created from 1838 to the present. Other society offerings include lectures, auctions and publications.

Address/Telephone: 128 East 63 Street (at Lexington Avenue), New York, NY 10021, (212) 838-2560

When to Visit: Tuesdays—10 A.M. to 8 P.M. Wednesdays–Fridays—10 A.M. to 5 P.M. Saturdays—noon to 4 P.M.

Days/Holidays Closed: August, Sundays, Mondays and all major holidays

Charges/Fees: Free

Suggested Grades: 3–adult

Guided Tour: Available upon request; 15 minutes

Maximum Group: 50

Group Notice: 1 week

Eating Facilities: None

Restroom Facilities: Yes

Handicapped Access: Limited to one of two galleries

Gift Shop: Yes

Library/Research Facilities: By appointment only (open one day a week)

By Subway: Nos. 4, 5 or 6 to 59 Street; No. 6 to 68 Street; B (according to schedule), N, Q or R to Lexington Avenue

By Bus: M98, M101 or M102

74 · SOLOMON R. GUGGENHEIM MUSEUM

Founded during the late 1920s by Solomon R. Guggenheim, the Guggenheim Museum has one of the world's largest collections of paintings by Kandinsky, as well as holdings of works by Brancusi, Calder, Chagall, Delaunay, Klee, Miró, Picasso and other major twentieth-century artists. It is housed in a building designed by Frank Lloyd Wright and opened in 1959—the only work by the famed architect that stands in Manhattan. In 1976 Justin K. Thannhauser bequeathed additional masterworks by Cézanne, Degas, Gauguin, Manet, Picasso, Toulouse-Lautrec, van Gogh and others. In 1990 the museum acquired the Panza di Biumo collection of over 200 works of American Minimalist art from the 1960s and 70s, making the museum's collection one of the most extensive holdings of twentieth-century art. The museum reopened in 1992, after a two-year restoration project. An addition by Gwathmey Siegel & Associates doubled the museum's exhibition space.

Address/Telephone: 1071 Fifth Avenue (at East 88 Street), New York, NY 10128, (212) 423-3500

When to Visit: Sundays–Wednesdays—10 A.M. to 6 P.M. Fridays and Saturdays—10 A.M. to 8 P.M.

Days/Holidays Closed: Thursdays

Charges/Fees: Adults—$7; seniors, students—$4; members and children under 12—free. On Fridays, from 6 P.M. to 8 P.M., pay what you wish

Suggested Grades: All grades

Guided Tour: By reservation only; 1 hour

Maximum Group: 50

Group Notice: 4–6 weeks (payment required in advance)

Eating Facilities: Yes

Restroom Facilities: Yes

Handicapped Access: Yes

Gift Shop: Yes

Library/Research Facilities: None

By Subway: Nos. 4, 5 or 6 to 86 Street

By Bus: M1, M2, M3, M4, M18 or M86

75 · SONY WONDER TECHNOLOGY LAB

Sony Wonder Technology Lab is an interactive science-and-technology center designed for students of all ages. At Sony Wonder, visitors explore state-of-the-art communications technology, taking a behind-the-scenes look at the inner workings of technological equipment and trying their hands at some of the exciting professions in the field of communications and technology.

Address/Telephone: 550 Madison Avenue (at East 56 Street), New York, NY 10022, (212) 833-8100

When to Visit: Tuesdays–Saturdays—10 A.M. to 6 P.M. Sundays—noon to 6 P.M.

Days/Holidays Closed: Mondays, New Year's Day, Easter Sunday, Thanksgiving and Christmas
Charges/Fees: Free
Suggested Grades: 3–adult
Guided Tour: Group tours; 1½–2 hours (for educational and community groups only)
Maximum Group: 40 (minimum group: 10)
Group Notice: 2 months

Eating Facilities: None
Restroom Facilities: Yes
Handicapped Access: Yes
Gift Shop: Yes
Library/Research Facilities: None
By Subway: E, F, N or R to Fifth Avenue; Nos. 4, 5 or 6 to 59 Street
By Bus: M1, M2, M3, M4, M5, M30, M31 or M57

76 · SOUTH STREET SEAPORT MUSEUM

The South Street Seaport Museum was founded in 1967 to preserve, interpret and display the history of New York City as a world port, highlighting both the South Street Seaport area and the tremendous contribution of maritime activity to the economic, social and cultural heritage of New York City and the nation. The museum occupies an 11-square-block Landmark Historic District, which also houses more than 100 shops and restaurants. The museum proper is made up of exhibition galleries, restored nineteenth-century buildings, a working nineteenth-century print shop, boat-building shop, maritime-crafts center, children's center, library, historic art and archaeological collections and two museum shops. The museum's fleet of historic ships include two National Historic Landmarks: the *Lettie G. Howard,* an 1893 wood Fredonia fishing schooner; and the *Ambrose,* a 1908 steel lightship. There is also a variety of programs developed and offered by the museum, including changing exhibitions, workshops and participatory exhibitions for children and families, school programs, historic-district and ship tours, films, lectures, maritime festivals, regattas and waterfront events.

Address/Telephone: 207 Front Street (at Fulton Street), New York, NY 10038, (212) 748-8600
When to Visit: Daily—10 A.M. to 5 P.M. Summer hours: Daily—10 A.M. to 6 P.M.
Days/Holidays Closed: January 2 and Christmas
Charges/Fees: Adults—$6; seniors—$5; students—$4; children under 12—$3; members—free
Suggested Grades: All grades
Guided Tour: Public tours of ships available daily at 2 P.M. and 3 P.M. Special group tours available by reservation only

Maximum Group: Varies
Group Notice: 1 week
Eating Facilities: Yes. Picnic facilities also available along the pier
Restroom Facilities: Yes
Handicapped Access: Yes
Gift Shop: Yes
Library/Research Facilities: By appointment only
By Subway: Nos. 2, 3, 4, 5, J, M or Z to Fulton Street; A or C to Broadway–Nassau Street; E to World Trade Center
By Bus: M15

77 · STATUE OF LIBERTY NATIONAL MONUMENT AND MUSEUM

The Statue of Liberty is the most famous of our national monuments. Designed and created by Frédéric Bartholdi, the statue has stood in New York Harbor on Liberty Island since 1886. Visitors to Liberty Island can climb 22 stories (354 steps) to Liberty's crown—the torch is no longer accessible—and see the interior structure as well as a panoramic view of the harbor. If the climb seems too daunting, visitors can take the elevator 11 stories to the pedestal. A museum there features exhibits on immigration and on the conception and construction of the statue itself. There are spectacular views of New York Harbor from the promenade, the colonnade and top levels of the pedestal.

Address/Telephone: Liberty Island, New York, NY 10004, (212) 363-3200

When to Visit: Daily—9:30 A.M. to 5 P.M. Extended hours during the summer

Days/Holidays Closed: Christmas

Charges/Fees: No admission fee to Liberty Island, but there is a charge for the ferry, operated by the Circle Line, (212) 269-5755

Suggested Grades: All grades

Guided Tour: Public tours are conducted periodically throughout the day by park rangers as staffing levels permit (April– October outdoors, November–March indoors). The tours are 30 minutes long and available on a first-come, first-served basis. A variety of programs are available for school groups. Call Education, at (212) 363-7620

Maximum Group: Depends on program

Group Notice: Depends on program

Eating Facilities: Yes

Restroom Facilities: Yes

Handicapped Access: Yes

Gift Shop: Yes

Library/Research Facilities: None

By Subway: Nos. 1 or 9 to South Ferry; N or R to Whitehall Street; Nos. 4 or 5 to Bowling Green

By Bus: M1, M6 or M15

78 · STUDIO MUSEUM IN HARLEM

The Studio Museum in Harlem is the premier center for the collection, interpretation and exhibition of the art of African-Americans and artists of the African diaspora. Founded in 1967, the museum publishes the principal literature in the field, provides a prestigious artist-in-residence program and conducts extensive education programs for school children and the general public. In 1987, the museum received accreditation with commendation from the American Association of Museums, making it the first accredited Black or Hispanic fine-arts museum in the country.

Address/Telephone: 144 West 125 Street, New York, NY 10027, (212) 864-4500

When to Visit: Wednesdays–Fridays—10 A.M. to 5 P.M. Saturdays and Sundays—1 P.M. to 6 P.M.

Days/Holidays Closed: Mondays and Tuesdays

Charges/Fees: Adults—$5; seniors, students—$3; children under 12—$1

Guided Tour: Tuesdays—school groups by appointment only (call for details). Fridays—10:30 A.M., noon and 2 P.M. Saturdays—1 P.M., 2:30 P.M. and 4 P.M.

Maximum Group: 30

Group Notice: 3 weeks

Eating Facilities: None

Restroom Facilities: Yes

Handicapped Access: Yes

Gift Shop: Yes

Library/Research Facilities: None

By Subway: Nos. 2, 3, 4, 5 or 6 to 125 Street

By Bus: M2, M7, M60, M100, M101, M102 or Bx15

79 · TRINITY CHURCH

The Parish of Trinity Church received a charter from William III of England in 1697 and on March 13, 1698 held its first service. The first church building was destroyed by fire; the second, completed in 1790, was demolished in 1839 because of structural defects. The third and present church, designed by Richard Upjohn in the neo-Gothic style, was consecrated in 1846. Today the parish is composed of Trinity Church—Manhattan's oldest church—and St. Paul's Chapel, built in 1766 and the oldest public building in continuous use in the city. The church's permanent exhibit portrays the interrelationship of Trinity Parish and New York City. It is divided into several sections: "A Colonial Church in a Colonial Society," "A New Church in a New Nation," "A Changing Church in a Changing World" and others. Among the items on display are documents, maps, newspapers, burial records, sermons, financial records, prints, photographs, diary excerpts, pew books, Communion silver and portraits.

Address/Telephone: Broadway and Wall Street, New York, NY 10006, (212) 602-0872

Mailing Address: 74 Trinity Place, New York, NY 10006

When to Visit: Mondays–Fridays—9 A.M. to 11:45 A.M.; 1 P.M. to 3:45 P.M. Saturdays—10 A.M. to 3:45 P.M. Sundays—1 P.M. to 3:45 P.M.

Charges/Fees: Free

Suggested Grades: 3–adult

Guided Tour: Daily tours available at 2 P.M. and by appointment

Maximum Group: 50

Group Notice: As far in advance as possible

Eating Facilities: Yes (cafeteria on second floor of 74 Trinity Place, in back of church). Picnic facilities in the churchyard

Restroom Facilities: Yes

Handicapped Access: Yes

Gift Shop: The Trinity Bookstore (74 Trinity Place)

Library/Research Facilities: Trinity Church's reference department can be reached by writing

By Subway: Nos. 1, 9, N or R to Rector Street; Nos. 2, 3, 4 or 5 to Wall Street

By Bus: M1 or M6

80 · UKRAINIAN MUSEUM

The Ukrainian Museum collects, preserves and displays objects of artistic or historic merit relating to Ukrainian life and culture. The museum maintains three collections—folk art, fine arts and historic archives. The largest, with over 8000 objects, is the folk-art collection, including full folk costumes from various regions of Ukraine—embroidered shirts, embroideries, ritual clothes, kilims and Ukrainian Easter eggs. The fine-arts collection contains paintings, drawings and sculptures by many Ukrainian artists who worked in Ukraine, Europe and the United States. The historical archives are distinguished by a photographic history of Ukrainian immigration to the United States during the last 100 years. The museum organizes three to four exhibitions a year, either from its collections or from objects borrowed from other museums or individuals. It also offers courses and workshops, open to adults and children alike, in traditional crafts. Community programs include lectures, concerts and films.

Address/Telephone: 203 Second Avenue (between East 12 and 13 Streets), New York, NY 10003, (212) 228-0110

When to Visit: Wednesdays–Sundays—1 P.M. to 5 P.M.

Days/Holidays Closed: Mondays, Tuesdays, Ukrainian Christmas (January 7), Easter Sunday and Ukrainian Easter Sunday, Memorial Day, July 4, Labor Day, Thanksgiving and Christmas

Charges/Fees: Adults—$1; seniors, students—$.50; children under 12—free

Suggested Grades: All grades

Guided Tour: By appointment only; 30–45 minutes (duration of tour changes depending on the season; during Easter season a film is included in the tour)

Maximum Group: 25–30

Group Notice: 2–3 weeks

Eating Facilities: None

Restroom Facilities: Yes

Handicapped Access: Yes

Gift Shop: Yes

Library/Research Facilities: By appointment only

By Subway: L, N, R, Nos. 4, 5 or 6 to 14 Street–Union Square; L to Third Avenue or to First Avenue

By Bus: M9, M14 or M15

Additional Information: The museum is located in an area called "Little Ukraine," within walking distance of SoHo and Greenwich Village. There are several restaurants within a four-block area, including several Ukrainian establishments.

81 · UNITED NATIONS

The United Nations Headquarters is located on several acres of parkland and sculpture gardens between First Avenue and the East River. Starting from the General Assembly building, guided tours (offered in 20 languages) conduct visitors through the complex, where they can see not only the day-to-day workings of the 185 member nations, but also the work of artists such as Marc Chagall, Henry Moore, Pablo Picasso and

Norman Rockwell. There are also works and artifacts donated by member nations, including a model of "Sputnik" and a moon rock carried to Earth by the Apollo 11 mission. The guides are members of an international staff who explain the work of the U.N. and its related organizations. The complex is legally an "international zone," with its own uniformed security force and postal administration.

Address/Telephone: First Avenue at East 46 Street, New York, NY 10017, (212) 963-7713

When to Visit: March–December: Daily— 9:15 A.M. to 4:45 P.M. January and February: Mondays–Fridays—9:15 A.M. to 4:45 P.M.

Days/Holidays Closed: Saturdays and Sundays during January and February, New Year's Day, Thanksgiving and Christmas. Call (212) 963-7713 for up-to-date information

Charges/Fees: Adults—$6.50; seniors, students—$4.50; children (grades 1–8)—$3.50

Suggested Grades: 1–adult (children under 5 not permitted on tour)

Guided Tour: Yes; 15 minutes to 1 hour

Maximum Group: 15. Reservations required for groups of 15 or more; call Group Programmes at (212) 963-4440. Special programs may be arranged for groups of 20 or more (high-school age and above); call (212) 963-7710 for information

Group Notice: Several weeks

Eating Facilities: Yes (coffee shop on the Public Concourse, open from 9:30 A.M. to 4:30 P.M., and the Delegates Dining Room, open weekdays for an early luncheon sitting; call (212) 963-7625 for more information

Restroom Facilities: Yes

Handicapped Access: Yes

Gift Shop: Yes

Library/Research Facilities: None

By Subway: Nos. 4, 5, 6 or 7 to 42 Street–Grand Central

By Bus: M15, M27, M42, M50 or M104

Additional Information: The walk east to the United Nations from the 42 Street–Grand Central subway stop may be too long for some, in which case the bus route is recommended

82 • WHITNEY MIDTOWN MUSEUM OF AMERICAN ART AT PHILIP MORRIS

The Whitney Museum of American Art presents temporary exhibitions of twentieth-century American art in the gallery and sculpture court in the headquarters of Philip Morris Company, Inc.

Address/Telephone: 120 Park Avenue (at East 42 Street), New York, NY 10017, (212) 878-2550

When to Visit: Mondays, Tuesdays, Wednesdays and Fridays—11 A.M. to 6 P.M. Thursdays—11 A.M. to 7:30 P.M.

Days/Holidays Closed: Saturdays, Sundays and major holidays

Charges/Fees: Free

Guided Tour: Yes (Wednesdays and Fridays at 1 P.M.); 30 minutes

Eating Facilities: None

Restroom Facilities: Yes

Handicapped Access: Yes

Gift Shop: None

Library/Research Facilities: None

By Subway: Nos. 4, 5, 6 or 7 to 42 Street–Grand Central

By Bus: M1, M2, M3, M4, M5, M18, M42 or M104

83 · WHITNEY MUSEUM OF AMERICAN ART

The Whitney Museum of American Art, founded by Gertrude Vanderbilt Whitney in 1930, is dedicated to purchasing and exhibiting works by living artists, often in the year of their making. The permanent collection of twentieth-century American art is one of the most comprehensive in the world, with more than 10,000 paintings, sculptures, photographs, prints and drawings. Temporary exhibitions at the Whitney range from historical surveys and in-depth retrospectives of major twentieth-century artists to group shows introducing new and relatively unknown artists. The museum's Biennial Exhibitions are highlights of the New York art scene.

Address/Telephone: 945 Madison Avenue (at East 75 Street), New York, NY 10021, (212) 570-3676

When to Visit: Wednesdays—11 A.M. to 6 P.M. Thursdays—1 P.M. to 8 P.M. Fridays–Sundays—11 A.M. to 6 P.M.

Days/Holidays Closed: Mondays, Tuesdays, New Year's Day, July 4, Thanksgiving and Christmas

Charges/Fees: Adults—$7; seniors (over 65), students (with ID)—$5; children under 12—free

Guided Tour: Yes; approximately 1 hour

Group Notice: Group tours should be scheduled through the Education Office, (212) 606-0395

Eating Facilities: Yes (Sarabeth's at the Whitney restaurant)

Restroom Facilities: Yes

Handicapped Access: Yes

Gift Shop: Yes

Library/Research Facilities: By appointment only; call (212) 570-3648

By Subway: No. 6 to 77 Street

By Bus: M1, M2, M3, M4, M18, M30, M72 or M79

84 · YESHIVA UNIVERSITY MUSEUM

Yeshiva University offers changing exhibitions from around the world—art and artifacts from such Jewish communities as those in Germany, Ethiopia, Turkey, Morocco, Israel and the United States. In addition, the museum has an extensive community-outreach program offering exhibitions and tours in Spanish, Russian, Yiddish and other languages, educational programs for both children and adults, and research materials for scholars.

Address/Telephone: 2520 Amsterdam Avenue (between West 185 and 186 Streets), New York, NY 10033, (212) 960-5390

When to Visit: Tuesdays–Thursdays—10:30 A.M. to 5 P.M. Sundays—noon to 6 P.M.

Days/Holidays Closed: Mondays, Fridays, Saturdays and all Jewish holidays

Charges/Fees: Adults—$3; seniors, children—$2; $60 for groups of 25; $120 for groups of 50

Suggested Grades: K–adult.

Guided Tour: Yes; 1 to 1½ hours

Maximum Group: 50

Group Notice: As far in advance as possible

Eating Facilities: Yes (university cafeteria). Picnic facilities available

Restroom Facilities: Yes

Handicapped Access: For some galleries

Gift Shop: Yes

Library/Research Facilities: Yes (university library)

By Subway: A, Nos. 1 or 9 to 181 Street

By Bus: M3, M18, M98, M101, Bx3, Bx11, Bx35 or Bx36

BRONX

93

Henry Hudson Pkwy.

Van Cortlandt Park

92

Broadway

91

Major Deegan Expwy.

90

Bronx Park

88

Bronx and Pelham Pkwy.

85

Shore Rd.

87

Cross Bronx Expwy.

Grand Concourse

86

Bruckner Expwy.

89

85 · BARTOW-PELL MANSION MUSEUM AND GARDENS

In 1654, an English physician, Thomas Pell, purchased a vast tract of land, including the site of the Bartow-Pell Mansion Museum. Pell's nephew and heir, Sir John Pell, built a manor house on the property in 1676. Several generations of the Pell family lived in this house, which was destroyed during the Revolutionary War. The present Greek Revival mansion was built in 1842 by Robert Bartow, whose grandfather, John, had married into the Pell family after the Revolutionary War. In 1888 it was purchased by the City of New York from the Bartow family, and over the next 25 years, the mansion and grounds decayed until 1914, when the site was saved by the International Garden Club. The Bartow-Pell mansion served as the home of the club until it opened as a public museum in 1946. Today the house and grounds have been restored to reflect a nineteenth-century lifestyle. The interior contains period furniture, decorative arts and paintings, a bed by Charles Honoré Lannuier and Neoclassical furniture attributed to Duncan Phyfe, Joseph Meeks and Sons, and others. There is a stone carriage house with a coach room, stable, hayloft and harness room, that now serves as a multipurpose interpretive facility. In addition to the cultivated land, meadows and wooded areas that surround the house much as they did in the nineteenth century, there are a walled garden, a formal fountain and an herb garden.

Address/Telephone: 895 Shore Road, Pelham Bay Park, Bronx, NY 10464, (718) 885-1461

When to Visit: Wednesdays, Saturdays and Sundays—noon to 4 P.M.

Days/Holidays Closed: Mondays, Tuesdays, Thursdays, Fridays, New Year's Day, Easter, Thanksgiving weekend and Christmas, last three weeks of August–Labor Day

Charges/Fees: Adults—$2.50; seniors—$1.25

Suggested Grades: 4–8

Guided Tour: Self-guided tours

Maximum Group: 40

Group Notice: 1–2 months

Eating Facilities: Luncheons available for group tours with advance reservations

Restroom Facilities: Yes

Handicapped Access: None

Gift Shop: None (but several books and a few items are offered for sale)

Library/Research Facilities: By appointment only

By Subway: No. 6 to Pelham Bay Park

By Bus: Westchester Bee line No. 45 to entrance gates (does not run on Sundays)

86 · BRONX MUSEUM OF THE ARTS

The Bronx Museum of the Arts was founded in 1971 as a county fine-arts museum to serve the ethnically diverse population of the Bronx. The museum exhibits twentieth-century and contemporary art in a central museum space and a network of satellite galleries. In 1986, the museum initiated a permanent collection of twentieth-century works of art concentrating on artists from, or culturally related to, Africa, Asia and Latin America. The museum's current collection contains more than 900 works of art, encompassing paintings, photographs, prints, drawings and mixed-media works on paper. The museum also offers a variety of arts-education programs for young children, artists and young adults, and weekend activities for children and adults, many of them free of charge.

Address/Telephone: 1040 Grand Concourse, Bronx, NY 10456, (718) 681-6000

When to Visit: Wednesdays—3 P.M. to 9 P.M. Thursdays–Fridays—10 A.M. to 5 P.M. Saturdays and Sundays—1 P.M. to 6 P.M.

Days/Holidays Closed: Mondays, Tuesdays, New Year's Day, Thanksgiving and Christmas

Charges/Fees: Suggested donation: adults—$3; seniors—$1; students—$2; children under 12 with an adult—free

Suggested Grades: All grades

Guided Tour: By appointment only

Eating Facilities: None

Restroom Facilities: Yes

Handicapped Access: Yes

Gift Shop: Yes

Library/Research Facilities: None

By Subway: C or D (according to schedule) or No. 4 to 161 Street–Yankee Stadium

By Bus: Bx1, Bx2 or BxM express

87 · BRONX ZOO

The Wildlife Conservation Society's Bronx Zoo is the largest urban zoo in the United States. Located on 265 acres of parkland, the zoo is home to over 4000 animals, including many endangered species. Open 365 days a year, the zoo has ten indoor exhibits and many outdoor habitats. Award-winning exhibits include "Jungle World," an Asian tropical rain forest; "Himalayan Highlands," home to the endangered snow leopard and the red panda; and "Baboon Reserve," a simulated journey through an archaeological dig with unexpected encounters with gelada baboons, rock hyrax and Nubian ibex. In the Children's Zoo, youngsters can experience the lives of animals by crawling through prairie-dog tunnels, climbing a spider's web, hopping like a wallaby and wearing a "turtle shell." Other highlights include the "World of Darkness," in which day turns into night for bats, flying foxes and naked mole rats, and the "World of Birds," which features two floors of aviaries.

Address/Telephone: Bronx River Parkway at Fordham Road, Bronx, NY 10460, (718) 367-1010

Mailing Address: 2300 Southern Boulevard, Bronx, NY 10460

When to Visit: April–October: Mondays–Fridays—10 A.M. to 5 P.M. Saturdays, Sundays and holidays—10 A.M. to 5:30 P.M. November–March: Daily—10 A.M. to 5 P.M.

Charges/Fees: Wednesdays—free. April 1–October 31: Adults—$6.75; seniors (over 65), children (2–12)—$3; children under 2—

free. November 1–March 31: Adults—$2.75; seniors, children—$2

Suggested Grades: All grades

Guided Tour: 1–1½ hour tours are available. Call Friends of Wildlife Conservation at (718) 220-5141

Maximum Group: 15 (recommended)

Group Notice: 2-week minimum

Eating Facilities: Yes (Lakeside Café; Zoo Terrace; Flamingo Pub; snack stands throughout the park). Picnic facilities available at Lakeside Café area or Zoo Terrace

Restroom Facilities: Yes

Handicapped Access: Yes

Gift Shop: Yes

Library/Research Facilities: Yes. Please call librarian/archivist in advance, (718) 220-6874

By Subway: No. 2 to Pelham Parkway or D to Fordham Road (Take Bx12 bus to Southern Boulevard and walk east to Fordham Road entrance)

By Bus: Bx9, Bx12 or Bx19

Additional Information: Alternative transportation from Manhattan to the zoo's Bronxdale Gate is provided by Liberty Lines bus service, (718) 652-8400, which stops along Madison Avenue and returns along Fifth Avenue. The park can also be reached by taking the Metro-North Commuter Railroad to Fordham Road, then taking the Bx9 to Southern Boulevard. Call (212) 532-4900 for information

A snow leopard and her cubs, the Bronx Zoo. *(Wildlife Conservation Society)*

88 · EDGAR ALLAN POE COTTAGE

Edgar Allan Poe spent the last period of his life—from 1846 to 1849—in the Bronx at Poe Cottage, now located at Kingsbridge Road and the Grand Concourse. A small wooden farmhouse built in 1812, the cottage once commanded unobstructed vistas of the rolling Bronx meadows to the shores of Long Island. Here the writer penned many of his most famous works, including "Annabel Lee," "The Bells" and *Eureka.* Shortly after Poe moved to the cottage with his wife Virginia for her health, she died of consumption. Poe himself died two years later in Baltimore. Administered by the Bronx County Historical Society since 1975, the cottage has been restored to its appearance during Poe's residence, with authentic period furnishings, including the bed in which Virginia died and the rocking chair Poe used, as well as other items. An audiovisual presentation and guided tour are provided.

Address/Telephone: Grand Concourse at East Kingsbridge Road (Poe Park and East 192 Street), Bronx, NY 10468, (718) 881-8900

Mailing Address: The Bronx County Historical Society, 3309 Bainbridge Avenue, Bronx, NY 10467

When to Visit: Open weekdays for group tours, by appointment only. Saturdays—10 A.M. to 4 P.M. Sundays—1 P.M. to 5 P.M.

Days/Holidays Closed: January and all major holidays

Charges/Fees: $2

Suggested Grades: All grades

Guided Tour: Yes; approximately 40 minutes

Maximum Group: 25–30

Group Notice: 2-week minimum

Eating Facilities: None. Picnic facilities are available in Poe Park

Restroom Facilities: In Poe Park

Handicapped Access: None

Gift Shop: Yes

Library/Research Facilities: By appointment only (3309 Bainbridge Avenue, Mondays–Fridays, 9 A.M. to 5 P.M.)

By Subway: No. 4 or D to Kingsbridge Road

By Bus: Bx1, Bx2, Bx9, Bx12, Bx17, Bx22, Bx28 or Bx34

89 · MARITIME INDUSTRY MUSEUM AT FORT SCHUYLER

Located on the campus of the State University of New York's Maritime College, the Maritime Industry Museum is housed in historic Fort Schuyler, which was completed in 1856. The museum offers one of the largest collections of maritime-industry-related items in the country and serves as a repository of books, periodicals, documents, papers, prints, photographs and old steamship-company records. The exhibition spaces are located on two floors, the upper floor dedicated to merchant marine exhibits and the lower floor housing exhibits on the history of the Maritime College, its training ships and twentieth-century passenger-ship lines. In addition to the main exhibit, "The Evolution of Seafaring," there are displays of famous eighteenth- and nineteenth-century naval battles fought in the United States, as well as exhibits on developing technologies in all aspects of shipping—from shipbuilding to navigational equipment—through different periods.

Address/Telephone: SUNY Maritime College Campus, 6 Pennyfield Avenue, Fort Schuyler Station, NY 10465, (718) 409-7218

When to Visit: Mondays–Saturdays—9 A.M. to 4 P.M. Sundays—noon to 4 P.M.

Charges/Fees: Free (donations accepted)

Guided Tour: Cadet tours available (Saturdays and Sundays). Group tours available; call (718) 409-7218

Maximum Group: Call (718) 409-7218 for information

Group Notice: Call (718) 409-7218 for information

Restroom Facilities: Yes

Gift Shop: Yes

Library/Research Facilities: Yes

By Subway: No. 6 to Westchester Square (take the Bx40 bus to Maritime College entrance, last stop)

By Bus: New York Bus Service (718-994-3500) operates an express bus (Throgs Neck express) to Fort Schuyler at Pennyfield and Harding Avenues, approximately ½ mile from campus

• MUSEUM OF BRONX HISTORY: see VALENTINE-VARIAN HOUSE

90 • NEW YORK BOTANICAL GARDEN

A National Historic Landmark, the New York Botanical Garden is set in 250 acres in the north Bronx. The garden was the project of Nathaniel Lord Britton and his wife Elizabeth, two botanists who were inspired by the Royal Botanic Gardens at Kew, near London. In 1891 they began raising funds and planning the gardens, which are now among the largest in the world. Among the horticultural attractions are 27 specialty gardens and plant collections, including the Peggy Rockefeller Rose Garden, the T. H. Everett Rock Garden, the Jane Watson Irwin Perennial Garden and collections of daylilies, orchids, ferns, flowering trees, conifers and pines. There is also the Enid A. Haupt Conservatory, a glass structure constructed in 1902 that was influenced by the famous Crystal Palace, and several other landmark buildings. Tours, daily trams, special events, a family garden and hands-on craft and nature activities are regularly scheduled. The New York Botanical Garden also sponsors scientific research and a variety of education programs.

Address/Telephone: 200 Street and Southern Boulevard, Bronx, NY 10458, (718) 817-8700

When to Visit: April–October: Tuesdays–Sundays (and Monday holidays)—10 A.M. to 6 P.M. November–March: Tuesdays–Sundays (and Monday holidays)—10 A.M. to 4 P.M.

Days/Holidays Closed: Mondays (except Monday holidays) and Christmas

Charges/Fees: Adults—$3; seniors, students,

children (6–16)—$1; children under 6—free. Free admission all day Wednesday and Saturday from 10 A.M. to noon

Suggested Grades: All grades

Guided Tour: A variety of tour options, including guided and self-guided tours, are available. Call the Adult Group Tour Office, (718) 817-8687, for information, fees and reservations

Maximum Group: Depends on tour

Group Notice: Depends on tour

Eating Facilities: Yes. Picnic facilities also available

Restroom Facilities: Yes

Handicapped Access: Yes

Gift Shop: Yes

Library/Research Facilities: Yes (open Tuesdays, Wednesdays and Thursdays, 9 A.M. to 5 P.M.; Fridays, 9 A.M. to 6 P.M.

By Subway: C, D or No. 4 to Bedford Park Boulevard (take Bx26 to main gate)

By Bus: Bx19 or Bx26

Additional Information: The Metro-North Botanical Garden station is directly across from the garden's main gate

91 · VALENTINE-VARIAN HOUSE/ MUSEUM OF BRONX HISTORY

Set in a park surrounded by fruit trees and a small colonial garden, the historic Valentine-Varian House lies half an hour by public transportation from the center of Manhattan. The four-level fieldstone farmhouse has stood since 1758, when Isaac Valentine built it near the Boston Post Road. It was later the site of six Revolutionary War skirmishes and was occupied by the British for most of the war. In 1791, the house passed into the hands of the Varian family, who owned it for the next 114 years. It changed hands once more in 1905, when William F. Beller purchased it. In 1965, the house was donated to the Bronx County Historical Society, and in 1968 the restored house was opened to the public as the Museum of Bronx History. The main floor serves as a permanent exhibition space where the museum displays objects from its collection of artifacts and photos; exhibitions document all periods of Bronx history from pre-Revolutionary days to the present.

Address/Telephone: 3266 Bainbridge Avenue (at East 208 Street), Bronx, NY 10467, (718) 881-8900

Mailing Address: The Bronx County Historical Society, 3309 Bainbridge Avenue, Bronx, NY 10467

When to Visit: Open weekdays for group tours, by appointment only. Saturdays—10 A.M. to 4 P.M. Sundays—1 P.M. to 5 P.M.

Days/Holidays Closed: January and all major holidays

Charges/Fees: $2

Suggested Grades: All grades

Guided Tour: Yes; 40 minutes

Maximum Group: 50

Group Notice: 2-week minimum

Eating Facilities: None

Restroom Facilities: Yes

Handicapped Access: None

Gift Shop: Yes

Library/Research Facilities: By appointment only (3309 Bainbridge Avenue, Mondays–Fridays, 9 A.M. to 5 P.M.)

By Subway: D to 205 Street; No. 4 to Mosholu Parkway

By Bus: Bx10, Bx28 or Bx34

92 · VAN CORTLANDT HOUSE MUSEUM

From 1748 to 1896, the Van Cortlandt family estate was a prosperous plantation, with extensive planting fields and livestock, a gristmill and a resident community of craftsmen and field workers, some free and some enslaved. Since 1896, the Van Cortlandt House has served as a museum, offering a view of plantation life in the lower Hudson River Valley. Listed in the National Register of Historic Places, the museum is furnished with decorative arts and Van Cortlandt family heirlooms from the Colonial and Federal periods. The museum also sponsors a wide range of public programs, including school programs, group tours, lectures and workshops.

Address/Telephone: Van Cortlandt Park (at Broadway near 246 Street), Bronx, NY 10471, (718) 543-3344

When to Visit: Tuesdays–Fridays—10 A.M. to 3 P.M. Saturdays and Sundays—11 A.M. to 4 P.M.

Days/Holidays Closed: Mondays, New Year's Day, Memorial Day, July 4, Labor Day and Christmas

Charges/Fees: Adults—$2; seniors, students—$1.50; children under 14—free

Suggested Grades: All grades

Guided Tour: Self-guided and prearranged group tours. Call (718) 543-3344 for information and reservations

Maximum Group: 50

Group Notice: 1 month

Eating Facilities: None. Picnic facilities available on fairgrounds

Restroom Facilities: Yes

Handicapped Access: Grounds are accessible, museum is not

Gift Shop: Yes

Library/Research Facilities: By appointment only

By Subway: Nos. 1 or 9 to 242 Street

By Bus: Bx9, Liberty Lines MxM3; Westchester Bee line Nos. 1, 2 or 3

93 · WAVE HILL

Often called the most beautiful place in New York, Wave Hill is a 28-acre public garden in a spectacular setting overlooking the Hudson River and Palisades. Built as a country home in 1843 by jurist William Lewis Morris, from 1866 to 1903 the house was owned by publishing scion William Henry Appleton, who brought to Wave Hill such famous natural scientists as Thomas Henry Huxley and Charles Darwin. (It has also been home to Theodore Roosevelt, Mark Twain and Arturo Toscanini.) In 1903 the estate was purchased by George W. Perkins, a partner of J. P. Morgan, who spent much time planning and enhancing the magnificent grounds. Since 1960 Wave Hill has been a property of the City of New York. Today visitors can enjoy the extensive grounds, gardens, greenhouses, historic buildings, lawns and woodlands. Wave Hill also offers programs in horticulture, environmental education, land management, landscape history and the arts.

Address/Telephone: West 249 Street and Independence Avenue, Bronx, NY 10471, (718) 549-3200

Mailing Address: 675 West 252 Street, Bronx, NY 10471

When to Visit: Mid-May–mid-October: Tuesdays–Sundays—9 A.M. to 5:30 P.M. Wednesdays—until dusk. Mid-October–mid-May: Tuesdays–Sundays—9 A.M. to 4:30 P.M. Holiday Mondays—call for specific times

Days/Holidays Closed: Mondays (except holiday weekends—call for a specific schedule), New Year's Day and Christmas

Charges/Fees: Weekdays—free. Weekends and holidays: adults—$4; seniors, students—$2; children under 6—free

Suggested Grades: All grades

Guided Tour: Yes (Sundays at 2:15 P.M.); 1–1½ hours

Maximum Group: 48, or one busload

Group Notice: As far in advance as possible

Eating Facilities: Yes (café). Picnic facilities also available

Restroom Facilities: Yes

Handicapped Access: Limited (call for information)

Gift Shop: Yes

Library/Research Facilities: None

By Subway/Bus: Nos. 1 or 9 subway to 231 Street; board Bx7 or Bx10 at the northwest corner of 231 Street, exit at 252 Street. Walk across parkway bridge and turn left to 249 Street. Turn right and continue to Wave Hill gate. Or, take the A subway to 207 Street (last stop); board Bx7 northbound bus to 252 Street and continue as above. Or, take the Bx1 or Bx9 to 231 Street and Broadway, transfer to Bx7 or Bx10 to 252 Street and follow walking directions as above

Additional Information: From Manhattan, Wave Hill can also be reached by Metro-North Commuter Railroad (212) 532-4900 and Liberty Lines Express Bus (212)/(718) 652-8400

A view of the Hudson River and Palisades from Wave Hill. *(Photograph by David Manning)*

BROOKLYN

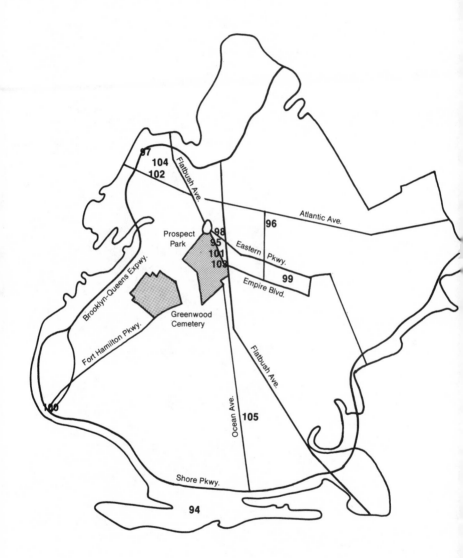

87
104
102
Flatbush Ave.

Atlantic Ave.

Prospect
Park

98
95
101
103

96

Eastern Pkwy.

99

Empire Blvd.

Brooklyn-Queens Expwy.

Greenwood
Cemetery

Fort Hamilton Pkwy.

Flatbush Ave.

100

Ocean Ave.

105

Shore Pkwy.

94

94 • AQUARIUM FOR WILDLIFE CONSERVATION

New York's Aquarium, part of the New York Zoological Society/Wildlife Conservation Society, is located on 14 acres beside the Atlantic Ocean at Coney Island, Brooklyn. The aquarium, whose collection contains over 10,000 marine life specimens, offers a variety of exhibits, including "Sea Cliffs," a replica of the Pacific coastline, which features above- and below-water viewing with winding corridors and panoramic underwater windows inside the exhibit, and rocks, trees and pools outside. It houses walruses, California sea otters, black-footed penguins and harbor, gray and fur seals. Four kinds of sharks swim with stingrays, lobsters and crabs in the 90,000-gallon shark exhibit. The Conservation Hall replicates various habitats, including the Belize Barrier Reef, the Amazon River, the Red Sea, Lake Victoria and Lake Malawi, focusing on the Wildlife Conservation Society's efforts in conservation. Six species of fish in this exhibit are endangered; five species are extinct in nature.

Address/Telephone: Surf Avenue and West 8 Street, Brooklyn, NY 11224, (718) 265-3474
When to Visit: Daily (365 days a year)—10 A.M. to 5 P.M.
Charges/Fees: Adults—$6.75; seniors, children (2–12)—$3; children under 2—free
Suggested Grades: All grades
Guided Tour: Yes; 2 hours
Maximum Group: Unlimited

Group Notice: 1 month
Eating Facilities: Yes (cafeteria and many snack bars). Picnic facilities available
Restroom Facilities: Yes
Handicapped Access: Yes
Gift Shop: Yes
Library/Research Facilities: Yes
By Subway: D or F to West 8 Street
By Bus: B36 or B68

95 • BROOKLYN BOTANIC GARDEN

More than 12,000 kinds of plants from around the world are displayed on the 52 acres and in the Steinhardt Conservatory of Brooklyn Botanic Garden. Among the specialty gardens are the Cranford Rose Garden, with over 5000 rosebushes of nearly 1200 varieties, and the herb garden, featuring a sixteenth-century Elizabethan love-knot design and medicinal, culinary, fragrant and ornamental herbs. Visitors can walk through the Steinhardt Conservatory's three pavilions featuring desert, tropical and warm temperate environments, in which a variety of plant species from around the world are exhibited. The C. V. Starr Bonsai Museum houses a collection with several bonsai well over 100 years old. A Japanese stroll garden is exceptionally picturesque. The spring display of cherry trees attracts thousands of visitors. The garden also offers an extensive education program for both adults and children and a variety of public programs featuring guided tours, local, national and international tours and other resources.

Address/Telephone: 1000 Washington Avenue (at Eastern Parkway), Brooklyn, NY 11225, (718) 622-4433

When to Visit: April–September: Tuesdays–Fridays—8 A.M. to 6 P.M. Saturdays, Sundays and holidays—10 A.M. to 6 P.M. October–March: Tuesdays–Fridays—8 A.M. to 4:30 P.M. Saturdays, Sundays and holidays—10 A.M. to 4:30 P.M.

Days/Holidays Closed: Mondays (except Monday holidays), New Year's Day, Thanksgiving and Christmas

Charges/Fees: Donations requested

Suggested Grades: All grades

Guided Tour: Free tours available weekends at 1 P.M. (except holiday weekends). Paid group tours available—(718) 622-4433 ext. 216 for information

Maximum Group: Depends on tour

Group Notice: Depends on tour

Eating Facilities: Yes (Terrace Café)

Restroom Facilities: Yes

Handicapped Access: Yes

Gift Shop: Yes

Library/Research Facilities: Yes

By Subway: D to Prospect Park; Nos. 2 or 3 to Eastern Parkway

By Bus: B41, B47 or B48

Cherry trees in bloom, Brooklyn Botanic Garden. *(Brooklyn Botanic Garden)*

96 · BROOKLYN CHILDREN'S MUSEUM

The Brooklyn Children's Museum is the world's first museum for young people. A collection of over 27,000 cultural artifacts and natural history specimens provides the basis for its interactive exhibitions and programs such as "Night Journeys," which features interactive environments in which visitors can try out life-size re-creations of beds from other cultures and hear lullabies from around the world. Other exhibitions include "Animals Eat," focusing on the eating habits of dozens of animals, and "The Mystery of Things," which invites children to solve mysteries by using their five senses. Museum instructors offer classes to school groups that supplement the New York State school curriculum, as well as workshops and special events for families and the general public.

Address/Telephone: 145 Brooklyn Avenue (at St. Marks Avenue), Brooklyn, NY 11213, (718) 735-4400

Mailing Address: Suite 520, 189 Montague Street, Brooklyn, NY 11201

When to Visit: Wednesdays–Fridays—2 P.M. to 5 P.M. Saturdays, Sundays and public-school holidays—noon to 5 P.M.

Days/Holidays Closed: Mondays and Tuesdays

Charges/Fees: Suggested donation—$3

Suggested Grades: All grades

Guided Tour: "Meet the Museum" is a 1-hour guided tour offered to school groups only on Fridays, 10 A.M. to 11 A.M. and from noon to 1 P.M. (limited to five classes per hour)

Maximum Group: 35 for school groups, otherwise no maximum

Group Notice: As far in advance as possible

Eating Facilities: None

Restroom Facilities: Yes

Handicapped Access: Yes

Gift Shop: None

Library/Research Facilities: Children's Resource Library

By Subway: No. 3 to Kingston Avenue; A or C to Kingston-Throop Avenues

By Bus: B44, B45 or B47

97 · BROOKLYN HISTORICAL SOCIETY

Founded in 1863, the Brooklyn (formerly Long Island) Historical Society is a museum, library and education center. The society is housed in a National Historic Landmark structure built by the organization in 1878–80. The extensive collection of Brooklyn-related research materials and artifacts ranges from seventeenth-century drawings to nineteenth-century paintings of ferryboats and Brooklyn landscapes. The society's permanent exhibition focuses on themes symbolic of the borough: the Brooklyn Bridge, the Brooklyn Navy Yard, the Brooklyn Dodgers, Coney Island and Brooklynites themselves. Community-related changing exhibits are often supplemented with oral histories and focus on important and topical issues. The society also offers a variety of public-education programs, including school programs with crafts, storytelling and puppet shows, as well as adult programming that features walking tours, lectures and concerts.

Address/Telephone: 128 Pierrepont Street (at Clinton Street), Brooklyn, NY 11201, (718) 624-0890

When to Visit: Museum: Tuesdays–Saturdays—noon to 5 P.M. Library: Tuesdays–Saturdays—noon to 4:45 P.M.

Days/Holidays Closed: Sundays, Mondays and national holidays

Charges/Fees: Museum and library members—free. Museum admission: adults—$2.50; seniors, children—$1; free admission on Wednesdays. Library admission: $5 (includes museum admission)

Suggested Grades: All grades

Guided Tour: By appointment only

Maximum Group: 35

Group Notice: 2 weeks

Eating Facilities: None

Restroom Facilities: Yes

Handicapped Access: Yes

Gift Shop: None

Library/Research Facilities: Yes (see above)

By Subway: Nos. 2, 3, 4 or 5 to Borough Hall; A, C or F to Jay Street–Borough Hall; M, N or R to Court Street

By Bus: B25, B26, B37, B41, B45, B52 or B61

98 · BROOKLYN MUSEUM

Housed in a six-story Beaux-Arts structure built in 1893, the museum contains approximately 1.5 million works of art. The museum's permanent collections are divided into six departments: Egyptian, Classical and Ancient Middle Eastern Art; African, Oceanic and New World Art; Asian Art; Decorative Arts, Costumes and Textiles; Prints, Drawings and Photographs; and Painting and Sculpture. In addition to its permanent collection, the museum offers a variety of special exhibits and special programs, including gallery talks, weekend drop-in programs for children, film and video series, lectures and a summer weekend jazz series in the museum's outdoor sculpture garden (home to a collection of architectural ornaments from demolished New York City buildings). The Art Reference Library, the Wilbour Library of Egyptology and the Brooklyn Museum Archives are open to the public for research purposes.

Address/Telephone: 200 Eastern Parkway (at Washington Avenue), Brooklyn, NY 11238, (718) 638-5000

When to Visit: Wednesdays–Sundays—10 A.M. to 5 P.M.

Days/Holidays Closed: Mondays, Tuesdays, New Year's Day, Thanksgiving and Christmas

Charges/Fees: Suggested donations: adults—$4; students (with ID)—$2; seniors—$1.50; members and children under 12 accompanied by an adult—free

Suggested Grades: All grades

Guided Tour: The museum offers a variety of tours of different durations. Call the Education Division at (718) 638-5000, ext. 221

Maximum Group: Depends on tour

Group Notice: 4 weeks

Eating Facilities: Yes (The Museum Café)

Restroom Facilities: Yes

Handicapped Access: Yes

Gift Shop: Main Brooklyn Museum Shop and artSmart Children's Shop. (There is also a museum shop at Equitable Tower, 787 Seventh Avenue, in Manhattan)

Library/Research Facilities: By appointment only (Art Reference Library and Wilbour Library of Egyptology)

By Subway: Nos. 2 or 3 to Eastern Parkway–Brooklyn Museum; D, Q or S to Prospect Park

By Bus: B41, B48, B69 or B71

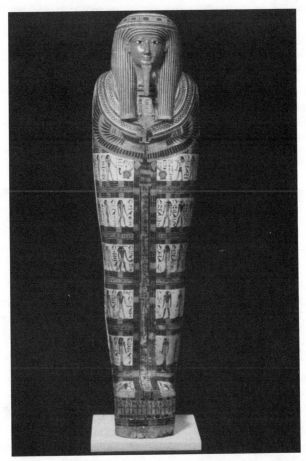

Mummy cartonnage, ca. 945–715 B.C., in the Brooklyn Museum.

99 · CHASSIDIC ART INSTITUTE

This institute and art gallery is located in the heart of the Crown Heights district of Brooklyn. Established in 1978—prompted by the success of a six-week exhibit of Chassidic art at the Brooklyn Museum—the institute is the world's first gallery featuring Chassidic art exclusively. The institute houses more than 100 paintings, sculptures and photographic works, and guests from around the world visit the galleries to view works by Chassidic artists, many of whom live and work in Crown Heights; some are recent Russian immigrants. The institute supports these artists by providing materials, supplies and exhibition space. In addition, the institute sponsors traveling exhibits and provides art instruction taught by trained Chassidic artists.

Address/Telephone: 375 Kingston Avenue, Brooklyn, NY 11213, (718) 774-9149
When to Visit: Sundays–Thursdays—noon to 7 P.M. Fridays—noon until 2 hours before sunset
Days/Holidays Closed: Saturdays and all Jewish holidays
Charges/Fees: Free
Suggested Grades: All grades
Guided Tour: 1 hour
Maximum Group: 30

Group Notice: 1 week
Eating Facilities: None
Restroom Facilities: Yes
Handicapped Access: None
Gift Shop: Yes
Library/Research Facilities: None
By Subway: No. 3 to Kingston Avenue
By Bus: B47
Additional Information: Exhibits are changed every six weeks

100 · HARBOR DEFENSE MUSEUM

The Harbor Defense Museum, in an 1825 flank battery of Fort Hamilton, is part of a National Register structure. Fort Hamilton served as part of New York City's defenses, and the Museum emphasizes the period from 1800 to 1950. Special exhibits cover other New York City–related military topics. A wall of cannons, dating from the eighteenth century to the Korean War, is located between the fort's gate and the museum.

Address/Telephone: Building 230, Fort Hamilton (entrance at 101 Street and Fort Hamilton Parkway), Brooklyn, NY 11252-5201, (718) 630-4349
When to Visit: Mondays–Fridays—1 P.M. to 4 P.M. Open Memorial Day, July 4 and Veterans Day
Days/Holidays Closed: Saturdays, Sundays and federal holidays not listed above and December 25–January 1
Charges/Fees: Free

Suggested Grades: 3–8
Guided Tour: Yes; 30 minutes
Maximum Group: 25 (children's groups require 1 adult for every 7 children)
Group Notice: 1 month
Eating Facilities: None; picnic facilities available in nearby park
Restroom Facilities: None
By Subway: R to 95 Street
By Bus: B8 or B16
Additional Information: Free off-street parking

101 · LEFFERTS HOMESTEAD

One of the few surviving Dutch Colonial farmhouses in Brooklyn, Lefferts Homestead (built 1777–83) is operated by the Prospect Park Alliance as a Children's Historic House Museum. The museum's exhibitions combine interactive toys and games with period rooms furnished in the style of the 1820s. Seasonal programs such as "Linen from Flax" involve children in the seasonal tasks of planting, harvest and textile production. There are also folk-art presentations and programs teaching children how historians learn about the past through archival documents and artifacts.

Address/Telephone: In Prospect Park at Flat-
bush Avenue (near Empire Boulevard),
Brooklyn, NY 11215, (718) 965-6505
Mailing Address: Lefferts Homestead, Prospect
Park Alliance, 95 Prospect Park West,
Brooklyn, NY 11215
When to Visit: Seasonal hours; please call for
up-to-date information
Charges/Fees: Free
Suggested Grades: All grades
Guided Tour: By reservation only; 45 to 90
minutes (depending on group's age-level and
interests)

Maximum Group: 30
Group Notice: 2 weeks
Eating Facilities: None; picnic facilities avail-
able nearby in Prospect Park
Restroom Facilities: None
Handicapped Access: In design phase
By Subway: D, Q or S to Prospect Park; Nos. 2
or 3 to Eastern Parkway
By Bus: B41, B47 or B48

• LONG ISLAND HISTORICAL SOCIETY: see BROOKLYN HISTORICAL SOCIETY

102 • NEW YORK TRANSIT MUSEUM

The New York Transit Museum is home to 100 years of transit lore and
memorabilia. It is located in an authentic 1930s subway station containing
19 vintage subway and elevated cars, antique turnstiles, a working signal
tower and a gift shop. Also offering lectures, behind-the-scenes transit
tours, walking tours and vintage bus displays, the museum is just over the
Brooklyn Bridge, five minutes from lower Manhattan.

Address/Telephone: Boerum Place and Scher-
merhorn Street, Brooklyn, NY 11201, (718)
330-3060 (information); (718) 330-8601
(museum operator)
Mailing Address: Room 9001, 130 Livingston
Street, Brooklyn, NY 11201
When to Visit: Tuesdays–Fridays—10 A.M. to
4 P.M. Saturdays and Sundays—noon to 5
P.M.
Days/Holidays Closed: Mondays and all major
holidays
Charges/Fees: Adults—$3; seniors, children—
$1.50
Suggested Grades: All grades. Call the museum
educator for information on special programs
(718) 330-8601
Guided Tour: Self-guided tours available.
Guided group tours often available
Maximum Group: 50
Group Notice: As far in advance as possible
(maximum 3 months); reservations may be

made any time and are required for groups.
Call (718) 330-3063 to schedule tours
Eating Facilities: Lunchroom with tables and
benches available for schoolchildren who
bring lunches
Restroom Facilities: Yes
Handicapped Access: None
Gift Shop: Yes (additional gift shop at Grand
Central Terminal)
Library/Research Facilities: Yes. Call Archives,
(718) 694-1068
By Subway: Nos. 2, 3, 4 or 5 to Borough Hall;
M, N or R to Court Street; A, C or G to
Hoyt–Schermerhorn Streets; A, C or F to Jay
Street–Borough Hall
By Bus: B25, B26, B37, B38, B41, B45, B52 or
B61
Additional Information: The Transit Museum
offers special weekend programs for children,
free with admission. Call (718) 694-5103
for a free calendar of events

103 · PROSPECT PARK WILDLIFE CENTER

Operated under the auspices of the Wildlife Conservation Society, the Prospect Park Wildlife Center is situated on 12 acres in Prospect Park. The recently renovated facility, targeted at children, is divided into three major exhibit areas: "The World of Animals," "Animal Lifestyles" and "Animals in Our Lives." The last-named area has up-close exhibits that highlight the beauty and form of animals; drawing supplies are provided so young visitors can sketch what they see. The exhibit also focuses on pets, and features a barnyard area where visitors can be close to sheep, goats and cows. The Animal Lifestyles building has indoor exhibits with glass-enclosed viewing areas and features animals ranging from weaver finches to garfish to the popular baboons. The World of Animals, comprised of outdoor exhibits stretching over two and a half acres, features a "Discovery Trail" where children can actually experience an animal's habitat. There are a variety of interactive exhibits, including the "Wallaby Walkabout," where visitors can walk freely among Australian wallabies. Also on the trail are other animals, including red panda, porcupine and capybara; the walk culminates in the center's aviary in which visitors can watch free-flying birds and explore the environment where they live.

Address/Telephone: 450 Flatbush Avenue, Brooklyn, NY 11225, (718) 399-7339
When to Visit: April–October: Mondays–Fridays—10 A.M. to 5 P.M. Saturdays, Sundays and holidays—10 A.M. to 5:30 P.M. November–March: Daily—10 A.M. to 4:30 P.M.
Charges/Fees: Adults—$2.50; seniors—$1.25; children (3–12)—$.50; children under 3—free
Suggested Grades: All grades
Guided Tour: Informal tours offered daily, once a day; 1 hour

Maximum Group: No maximum
Group Notice: None required
Eating Facilities: Yes
Restroom Facilities: Yes
Handicapped Access: Yes
Gift Shop: Yes
Library/Research Facilities: None
By Subway: D, Q or S (Franklin Avenue Shuttle) to Prospect Park (walk north on Flatbush Avenue to Center entrance)
By Bus: B41, B47 or B48

104 · ST. ANN AND THE HOLY TRINITY EPISCOPAL CHURCH

Recently designated a National Historic Landmark, St. Ann and the Holy Trinity Episcopal Church was designed in 1844 by Minard Lafever to rival Manhattan's Trinity Church. The church houses the first figural stained-glass windows made in America, designed by Jay Bolton between 1844 and 1846. In order to preserve and restore the church's 60 windows, the St. Ann's Stained Glass Conservation Studio was established. To date, five windows have been restored, including one that is on permanent loan to the Metropolitan Museum of Art. Visitors to the studio can view restorers and apprentices at work on the windows.

Address/Telephone: 157 Montague Street (at Clinton Street), Brooklyn, NY 11201, (718) 875-6960

Mailing Address: Second floor, 157 Montague Street, Brooklyn, NY 11201

When to Visit: Parish office hours: Mondays–Fridays—9 A.M. to 4 P.M. Stained Glass Studio: Mondays–Fridays—9 A.M. to 4 P.M. (or by appointment). Church: Mondays–Fridays—noon to 2 P.M.

Charges/Fees: Stained Glass Studio: Suggested donation—$3. Church—donations welcome

Suggested Grades: Stained Glass Studio: 3–adult. Church: all grades

Guided Tour: School groups and others by appointment; 15 minutes to 1 hour

Maximum Group: None

Group Notice: 1 month preferred; 1-week minimum

Eating Facilities: None

Restroom Facilities: Yes

Handicapped Access: Limited (to church only)

Gift Shop: None

Library/Research Facilities: None

By Subway: N or R to Court Street; Nos. 2, 3, 4, 5 to Borough Hall; A, C or F to Jay Street–Borough Hall

By Bus: B25, B26, B37, B41, B45, B52 or B61

105 · WYCKOFF HOUSE MUSEUM

Dating from 1652, the Wyckoff House is the oldest building in New York State. It is a prime example of Dutch Colonial architecture, and stood on a 400-acre farm. Today it is an educational resource for schoolchildren studying colonial history. The museum is furnished with both antique and reproduction items as a typical seventeenth- to eighteenth-century farmhouse. The reproductions provide an opportunity for extensive hands-on experience of domestic colonial activities. The museum is situated in the center of a $1\frac{1}{3}$-acre grass park, which contains a black-walnut tree, peach tree, kitchen garden and a hedge of beach plums.

Address/Telephone: 5816 Clarendon Road (at Ralph Avenue), Brooklyn, NY 11203, (718) 629-5400

Mailing Address: P.O. Box 100-376, Brooklyn, NY 11210

When to Visit: April–October: Thursdays and Fridays—noon to 5 P.M. November–March: Thursdays and Fridays—noon to 4 P.M. Open for group tours by appointment

Days/Holidays Closed: Mondays, Tuesdays, Wednesdays, Saturdays and Sundays

Charges/Fees: Adults—$2; seniors, children—$1. Group programs—$45 per group (up to 30 people)

Suggested Grades: K–8 (especially recommended for 4th graders)

Guided Tour: Yes; 1½–2 hours

Maximum Group: 30

Group Notice: 2 weeks

Eating Facilities: None. Picnic facilities available

Restroom Facilities: None

Handicapped Access: Limited

By Subway/Bus: D or Q to Newkirk Avenue in Brooklyn, then board the B8 bus to the intersection of Beverly Road and East 59 Street, one block south from museum entrance

QUEENS

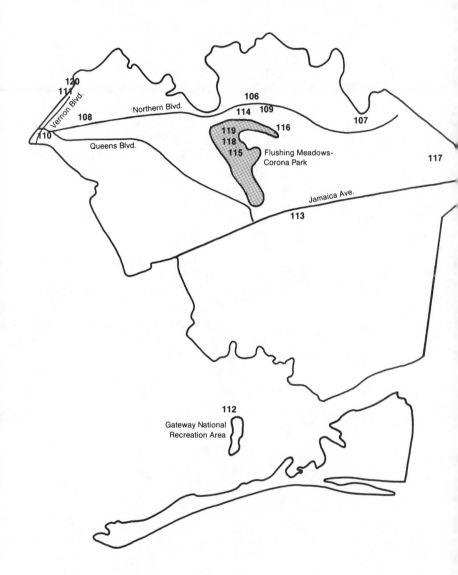

Vernon Blvd.

120
111
108
110

Northern Blvd.

106

114 109

116

Queens Blvd.

119
118
115

Flushing Meadows-
Corona Park

107

117

Jamaica Ave.

113

112

Gateway National
Recreation Area

106 · 1694 FRIENDS' MEETING HOUSE

In 1694 a Meeting House was built in Flushing by members of the Religious Society of Friends, or the Quakers, who had met with persecution at the hands of the Dutch when they held the area. John Bowne, who had invited the Quakers to worship in his house, had been imprisoned in New Amsterdam and then banished from the colony for his convictions; however, the governors of the West India Company in the Netherlands allowed him to return to his home (establishing, in effect, a policy of religious toleration), where the Quakers resumed their meetings. New Amsterdam fell to the English in 1664, becoming New York. After several years, the decision was made to raise a Meeting House, which is still in use today as a house of worship. The structure, the oldest house of worship in New York State, is a New York City Landmark and is listed in the National Register of Historic Places. (Bowne is buried in the Meeting House's cemetery.)

Address/Telephone: 137-16 Northern Boulevard (off Main Street), Queens, NY 11354, (718) 358-9636

When to Visit: Open by appointment and the first Sunday of every month from 12:30 P.M. to 1:30 P.M.

Charges/Fees: Free (donations welcome)

Suggested Grades: 4–adult

Guided Tour: Yes; 20–40 minutes (depending on group)

Maximum Group: 40

Group Notice: 4–6 weeks preferred

Eating Facilities: None

Restroom Facilities: Yes

Handicapped Access: Limited (there is only one step up into the Meeting House, but the restrooms are not wheelchair-accessible)

Gift Shop: None

Library/Research Facilities: None

By Subway: No. 7 to Main Street, Flushing

By Bus: Q12, Q13, Q14, Q15, Q16, Q17, Q20, Q26, Q27, Q28, Q44, Q48, Q65 or Q66

Additional Information: The Friends' Meeting House is part of the Flushing Freedom Mile Tour of historic sites. There is a self-guided walking tour or a guided tour of three houses (Kingsland, Bowne House and the Friends' Meeting House) on the tour. Contact the Queens Historical Society for more information, (718) 939-0647

107 · ALLEY POND ENVIRONMENTAL CENTER, INC.

The Alley Pond Environmental Center (APEC) was founded in 1972 to provide local educators with a living learning laboratory for students and adults. Over 635 acres of woodlands, meadows and fresh- and saltwater marshes encompass this park in northeast Queens. The center offers a variety of exhibits, including a small zoo and aquarium, as well as nature walks, craft workshops, shows, children's programs and special seasonal events.

Address/Telephone: 228-06 Northern Boulevard, Queens, NY 11363-1890, (718) 229-4000

When to Visit: Mondays–Fridays—9 A.M. to 4 P.M. Saturdays and Sundays—9:30 A.M. to 3:30 P.M. Summer hours: Tuesdays–Saturdays—9 A.M. to 4 P.M.

Days/Holidays Closed: Sundays, Mondays (during the summer), New Year's Day, Easter, Memorial Day, July 4, Labor Day, Thanksgiving and Christmas

Charges/Fees: Free (program fees vary)

Suggested Grades: All grades

Guided Tour: None

Maximum Group: 40

Group Notice: School groups should make reservations in September; other groups, 3–4 months in advance

Eating Facilities: Picnic facilities available

Restroom Facilities: Yes

Handicapped Access: Building, yes; park, no

Gift Shop: Yes

Library/Research Facilities: Limited

By Subway: No. 7 to Main Street, Flushing

By Bus: Q12

Tut's Fever Movie Palace, by Red Grooms and Lysiane Luong, American Museum of the Moving Image. *(Photograph by David Sunderberg/American Museum of the Moving Image)*

108 · AMERICAN MUSEUM OF THE MOVING IMAGE

The American Museum of the Moving Image is the only museum in the nation dedicated exclusively to motion pictures, television, video and digital media, contributing to the public's understanding through the collection and preservation of the material culture of the moving image. The museum offers exhibitions, film and video screenings and installations, lectures, seminars, tours for students, teacher workshops, specially commissioned artworks and a collection of over 70,000 artifacts related to film and television culture, such as film and television costumes, equipment, photographs, scale models and interactive displays.

Address/Telephone: 35 Avenue at 36 Street, Queens, NY 11106, (718) 784-0077

When to Visit: Tuesdays–Fridays—noon to 4 P.M. Saturdays and Sundays—noon to 6 P.M.

Days/Holidays Closed: Mondays and some holidays

Charges/Fees: Adults—$5; seniors—$4; children, students (with valid ID)—$2.50

Suggested Grades: 3–adult

Guided Tour: Guided tours of a 1–1½ hours for students. Must be reserved

Maximum Group: 30 students (1 adult for every 7 students required)

Group Notice: 2-week minimum

Eating Facilities: Yes (café area with vending machines). Picnic facilities available in café area

Restroom Facilities: Yes

Handicapped Access: Yes

Gift Shop: Yes

Library/Research Facilities: None

By Subway: G or R to Steinway Street or N to Broadway

By Bus: Q101

109 · BOWNE HOUSE

The Bowne House was built in 1661 by John Bowne, an immigrant from England. (See 1694 Friends' Meeting House, Queens.) Today it is considered one of the finest examples of vernacular Dutch-English architecture in the United States and contains a notable collection of seventeenth-, eighteenth- and nineteenth-century furniture, portraits and household objects, all of which belonged to the Bowne family. Among the highlights of the interior are the huge hearth with a seventeenth-century beehive oven, and a parlor, added in 1680, which has the original oak pegged floors and hand-hewn beams. Bowne's descendants also added to the original structure, including the present entry and a front parlor built by John's son Samuel, which features eighteenth-century wood paneling (with a Cross and Bible motif), a built-in china cabinet and other furniture. In 1945 the house was purchased by the Bowne House Historical Society, which continues to maintain and administer the house museum, as well as conducting educational programs.

Address/Telephone: 37-01 Bowne Street (at 37 Avenue), Queens, NY 11354, (718) 359-0528

When to Visit: Tuesdays, Saturdays and Sundays—2:30 P.M. to 4:30 P.M. School tours daily at 10 A.M. (By appointment only; call Education Programming (718) 359-0871.) All other times by appointment

Days/Holidays Closed: Mid-December–mid-January, all major holidays

Charges/Fees: Adults—$2; seniors, children under 12—$1; members—free

Suggested Grades: 3–7

Guided Tour: Yes; school tours last 1½ hours

Maximum Group: 30

Group Notice: Reservations required. Call Education Programming, (718) 359-0873

Eating Facilities: Picnic facilities available in park next door

Restroom Facilities: None

Handicapped Access: Yes

Gift Shop: Yes

Library/Research Facilities: By appointment only

By Subway: No. 7 to Main Street, Flushing

By Bus: Q13 or Q28

Additional Information: Call (718) 359-0528 for directions by car

110 · INSTITUTE FOR CONTEMPORARY ART P.S. 1 MUSEUM

The second exhibition space operated by the Institute for Contemporary Art (the other being the Clocktower Gallery in Manhattan; see under Institute for Contemporary Art, No. 37, in the Manhattan section), P.S. 1 Museum has produced surveys of the work of major artists. Exhibitions have included shows that might not have otherwise reached the New York metropolitan audience. The museum houses permanent installations of works by John Ahearn, Dennis Oppenheim, Alan Saret, Richard Serra and Richard Thatcher.

Address/Telephone: 46-01 21 Street, Queens, NY 11101, (718) 784-2084

When to Visit: Exhibition hours: Wednesdays–Sundays—noon to 6 p.m.

Days/Holidays Closed: Mondays, Tuesdays and all national holidays

Charges/Fees: Suggested donation—$2

Suggested Grades: 4–adult

Guided Tour: By appointment only (call Education Director for more information)

Maximum Group: 50

Group Notice: 2-week minimum

Eating Facilities: None

Restroom Facilities: Yes

Handicapped Access: Available in early 1996

Gift Shop: Yes

Library/Research Facilities: None

By Subway: E or F to 23 Street–Ely Avenue; No. 7 to 45 Road–Court House Square; G to Court Square

By Bus: Green Bus Lines, Q32, Q60 or Q101

111 · ISAMU NOGUCHI GARDEN MUSEUM

The museum houses a comprehensive collection of artworks by internationally renowned sculptor Isamu Noguchi (1904–1988). The museum includes 12 galleries and an outdoor sculpture garden with 24,000 square

~samu Noguchi Garden Museum. *(Photograph by Shigeo Anzai)*

feet of display space. On permanent exhibit at the museum are over 250 sculptures of stone, wood, metal and paper, as well as models, drawings and photo-documentation of Noguchi's many gardens and plazas. Also on display are stage sets designed for dances by Martha Graham, and Noguchi's paper light sculptures called *akari*. Originally a photoengraving plant, the building was converted by Noguchi for use as a studio and museum space.

Address/Telephone: 32-37 Vernon Boulevard, Queens, NY 11106, (718) 204-7088

When to Visit: April–November: Wednesdays, Saturdays and Sundays—11 A.M. to 6 P.M.

Days/Holidays Closed: December–March, Mondays, Tuesdays, Thursdays and Fridays

Charges/Fees: Suggested donations: adults—$4; seniors, students—$2

Suggested Grades: 2–adult

Guided Tour: Yes (2:00 P.M. on days museum is open); 1 hour. Private tours available upon request

Maximum Group: 40

Group Notice: 1 month

Eating Facilities: None

Restroom Facilities: Yes

Handicapped Access: First floor only

Gift Shop: Yes

Library/Research Facilities: By appointment only

By Subway: N to Broadway in Astoria, Queens

By Bus: Q104

Additional Information: The museum offers a weekend shuttle bus from Manhattan. Buses depart from Park Avenue and East 70 Street on the half hour on Saturdays and Sundays, beginning at 11:30 A.M. $5 for round-trip

112 · JAMAICA BAY WILDLIFE REFUGE

The Jamaica Bay Wildlife Refuge is nationally and internationally renowned as a prime resting spot where thousands of water, land and shorebirds stop each year during migration. Visitors can explore the diverse habitats of the refuge by walking along five miles of trails. Park rangers give interpretive talks and lead nature walks on a year-round basis; evening walks, birding workshops and a host of other programs are offered on a seasonal basis.

Address/Telephone: Cross Bay Boulevard, 1½ miles south from North Channel Bridge, Queens, NY, (718) 318-4340

Mailing Address: Jamaica Bay Wildlife Refuge, Gateway National Recreation Area, Building 69, Floyd Bennett Field, Brooklyn, NY 11234

When to Visit: Daily—8:30 A.M. to 5 P.M.

Days/Holidays Closed: New Year's Day, Thanksgiving and Christmas

Charges/Fees: Free

Suggested Grades: 3–6

Guided Tour: Yes; 2 hours

Maximum Group: School groups, 34

Group Notice: Advance reservations required. Reservations for fall taken after Labor Day; reservations for spring taken after January 1. Teacher workshop is required prior to visit

Eating Facilities: None. Picnic facilities available

Restroom Facilities: In Visitor Center

Handicapped Access: Yes, in Visitor Center (getting around grounds is difficult)

Gift Shop: Small bookstore in Visitor Center

Library/Research Facilities: None

By Subway: A to Broad Channel, then a 1-mile walk (approximately 15 minutes) to refuge

By Bus: Q21. The Green Bus Lines' Q21 stops at the Broad Channel station. Call (718) 474-9459 for schedule information

113 · KING MANOR MUSEUM

King Manor sits in the center of an 11-acre historic park in Jamaica, Queens. The house was the country residence and farm of Rufus King, statesman, diplomat, gentleman farmer, one of the signers of the United States Constitution and a staunch spokesman against slavery. Today the manor house has been restored to reflect King's tenancy in the early nineteenth century. Visitors can tour the library that originally held King's 5000-volume collection and read pages from his diary, account books and letters. There are also galleries devoted to local history and to village life in Jamaica in the early nineteenth century. In addition, the museum offers a variety of public programs as part of its community outreach.

King Manor Museum. *(Photograph © Sarah Wells 1989)*

Address/Telephone: King Park, 153 Street and Jamaica Avenue, Queens, NY 11432, (718) 206-0545

Mailing Address: Suite 704, 90-04 161 Street, Queens, NY 11432-6103

When to Visit: Saturdays and Sundays—12 P.M. to 4 P.M. Second and last Tuesday of each month—12:15 P.M. to 2 P.M. School and special-interest groups by appointment. A full series of public programs is offered during lunchtime on weekdays and on weekends (call for calendar of events)

Charges/Fees: Suggested donations: adults— $2; children—$1

Suggested Grades: 4–adult

Guided Tour: Yes; 1 hour

Maximum Group: 25 adults or 1 class

Group Notice: 3–4 weeks

Eating Facilities: None. Picnic facilities available in King Park (with children's playground and other amenities)

Restroom Facilities: Yes

Handicapped Access: Limited

Gift Shop: A few gift items are available for sale

Library/Research Facilities: None

By Subway: E, J or Z to Jamaica Center, walk one block west on Jamaica Avenue; F or R to Parsons Boulevard and Hillside Avenue, walk south on Parsons to Jamaica Avenue

By Bus: Q24, Q42, Q43, Q44, Q54, Q56 or Q83

Additional Information: King Manor can be reached via the Long Island Rail Road to Jamaica Station. Walk east 4 blocks from train station. King Manor is also easily reached by car and parking is available at nearby attended lots and a municipal garage; there is also limited metered parking on surrounding streets

114 · KINGSLAND HOMESTEAD QUEENS HISTORICAL SOCIETY

The late eighteenth-century Kingsland Homestead, home of the Queens Historical Society, stands in a small park in Flushing. The house, with its gambrel roof, side gable and Dutch door, was built around 1785 by Charles Doughty, the son of a wealthy Quaker. The name "Kingsland" derives from Doughty's son-in-law, British sea captain Joseph King, who bought the home in 1801. Today the first floor is used for exhibits on Queens history, drawing on the Historical Society's collection and other community resources. A second-floor parlor is decorated as if it belonged to a middle-class Victorian family, and personal mementos such as lacework, notebooks and eyeglasses belonging to the house's original owners are periodically displayed. In addition to maintaining Kingsland, the Queens Historical Society mounts a regular series of history-related exhibitions and lecture series in its gallery space. It also conducts walking tours of the borough.

Address/Telephone: 143-35 37 Avenue (at Parsons Boulevard), Queens, NY 11354, (718) 939-0647

When to Visit: Tuesdays, Saturdays and Sundays—2:30 P.M. to 4:30 P.M.

Days/Holidays Closed: Christmas Day through New Year's Day

Charges/Fees: Adults—$2; seniors, students—$1; Historical Society members—free

Suggested Grades: 4–adult

Guided Tour: Yes; 1 hour

Maximum Group: 15–20

Group Notice: 2–3 weeks

Eating Facilities: None. Picnic facilities available in the park

Restroom Facilities: Yes

Handicapped Access: Yes

Gift Shop: Bookstore

Library/Research Facilities: By appointment only (Mondays–Saturdays, 9:30 A.M. to 4:30 P.M.)

By Subway: No. 7 to Main Street, Flushing

By Bus: Q12, Q13, Q14, Q15, Q16, Q17, Q20, Q26, Q27, Q28, Q44, Q48, Q65 or Q66

Additional Information: For school group tours, one adult for every 10 children is required

Children enjoy a hands-on exhibit at the New York Hall of Science. *(Photograph by Teri Bloom)*

115 · NEW YORK HALL OF SCIENCE

New York City's hands-on science and technology center features over 150 activities and five permanent exhibitions. The largest of these is "Seeing the Light," an exploration of the world of color, light and perception, sponsored by the IBM Corporation and designed and built by the Exploratorium in San Francisco. Other exhibitions include "Sound-Sensations—The Inside Story of Audio," which explains aspects of audio technology such as compact discs, and "Realm of the Atom," featuring the world's first three-dimensional model of a hydrogen atom—magnified a billion times. "Hidden Kingdoms—the World of Microbes" is the nation's largest interactive microbiology exhibition. This exhibit focuses on the millions of microorganisms around us and how they affect our health and environment. In addition to family weekend workshops, the Hall of Science operates a multimedia library—the Science Access Center—that features an extensive collection of books, periodicals and videos; Science

Link is a series of interactive computer-based science education modules. The Hall of Science's staff, or Explainers, are on hand to interpret exhibits and present live science demonstrations daily.

Address/Telephone: 47-01 111 Street (at 48 Avenue), Flushing Meadows–Corona Park, Queens, NY 11368, (718) 699-0005

When to Visit: Wednesdays–Sundays—10 A.M. to 5 P.M. Groups only: Mondays and Tuesdays—10 A.M. to 2 P.M.

Days/Holidays Closed: New Year's Day, Thanksgiving and Christmas

Charges/Fees: Call for admission prices

Suggested Grades: All grades

Guided Tour: None

Eating Facilities: Yes (snack automat). Picnic facilities available

Restroom Facilities: Yes

Handicapped Access: Yes

Gift Shop: Yes

Library/Research Facilities: Yes

By Subway: No. 7 to 111 Street

By Bus: Q23 or Q48

• P.S. 1 MUSEUM: *see* INSTITUTE FOR CONTEMPORARY ART

116 • QUEENS BOTANICAL GARDEN

Queens Botanical Garden is located on 38 acres, 16 of which are cultivated as outdoor exhibits. The remaining acreage is an arboretum. The grounds feature rose, herb, rock, backyard and bird gardens (displaying plants that provide birds with food, shelter and nesting materials). There is also a woodland garden, a bee garden with live bees in hives, seasonal bulb and annual displays and a Victorian-style wedding garden. The Education Department offers a wide variety of programs for school groups in all grades. There are also seminars and curricula for advanced and secondary-school students and teacher training.

Address/Telephone: 43-50 Main Street (at Dahlia Avenue), Queens, NY 11355, (718) 886-3800

When to Visit: Mid-October–mid-April: Tuesdays–Sundays—10 A.M. to 4:30 P.M. Mid-April–mid-October: Tuesdays–Sundays—9 A.M. to 7 P.M.

Days/Holidays Closed: Mondays (except Monday holidays), New Year's Day, Thanksgiving and Christmas

Charges/Fees: General admission—free (call for information on various tour/school-program fees)

Suggested Grades: All grades

Guided Tour: Yes; 1½ hours ($50 fee, some free if prescheduled)

Maximum Group: 32

Group Notice: 2-week minimum. During the school year, it is recommended to call as early as possible (September or October) to secure the desired date

Eating Facilities: None. Limited picnic facilities available in arboretum area (no tables)

Restroom Facilities: Yes

Handicapped Access: Yes

Gift Shop: Plant shop open Wednesdays–Sundays—10 A.M. to 5 P.M.

Library/Research Facilities: None

By Subway/Bus: No. 7 to Main Street, Flushing, then Q44

117 · QUEENS COUNTY FARM MUSEUM

The Queens County Farm Museum is a 47-acre working farm in New York City consisting of the historic Adriance Farmhouse and its outbuildings, an orchard, a farmyard with livestock and planting fields. This landmark-designated site is the only remaining vestige of New York City's once-thriving agrarian past and is New York State's longest continuously farmed site. The museum interprets agriculture as a way of life from Colonial times to the present. Since 1976 the Farm Museum's educational programs and public events have provided audiences from throughout the tri-state area with valuable and unique programs, workshops and lectures, and give many urban visitors their first contact with agrarian life. Activities such as apple-pressing workshops, egg-incubation programs and the Hand-on-Farm tour enable visitors to experience a touch of farm life. County fairs, Indian pow-wows and craft exhibitions give visitors a day in the country without leaving New York City.

Address/Telephone: 73-50 Little Neck Parkway (at Union Turnpike), Queens, NY 11004, (718) 347-3276

When to Visit: Mondays–Fridays—9 A.M. to 5 P.M. Saturdays and Sundays—noon to 5 P.M.

Days/Holidays Closed: New Year's Day, Easter Sunday, Memorial Day, Labor Day, Columbus Day, Thanksgiving and Christmas

Charges/Fees: General admission—free. Some special events have a small entrance fee. School-group programs require reservations and fees, which vary according to the program

Suggested Grades: K–8

Guided Tour: Yes (on weekends and for school groups during the week); 45 minutes

Maximum Group: General, 35; school groups, 100 (with 2 tour guides)

Group Notice: 2 months (spring reservations require 3–4 months' notice)

Eating Facilities: None (corporate gatherings can be prearranged)

Restroom Facilities: Yes

Handicapped Access: Yes

Gift Shop: Yes

Library/Research Facilities: None

By Subway/Bus: E or F to Union Turnpike-Kew Gardens station, then Q46 to Little Neck Parkway; walk north 3 blocks to museum entrance

· QUEENS HISTORICAL SOCIETY: see KINGSLAND HOMESTEAD

118 · QUEENS MUSEUM OF ART

Established in 1972, the Queens Museum of Art is situated in the north wing of the New York City Building, one of the few structures remaining from the 1939 and 1964 World's Fairs. The museum has recently undergone extensive renovation to expand its facilities. Featuring changing exhibitions of twentieth-century and contemporary art, it also displays two permanent exhibitions focusing on the two World's Fairs. Built for the 1964 fair and recently updated, "Panorama of New York City" is an exact replica of all five boroughs of the city, spanning over 9000 square feet and featuring 865,000 buildings. "A Panoramic View: The History of the New York City Building" showcases both the 1939 and 1964 World's Fairs' archives and documents the history of the museum's site, from a Native American settlement to its present use. A third permanent exhibit features a selection of plaster casts of Classical and Renaissance sculpture, on loan from the Metropolitan Museum of Art. The museum also offers educational and public programming for children and adults, lectures, seminars and film and video screenings.

Address/Telephone: New York City Building, Flushing Meadows–Corona Park, Queens, NY 11368, (718) 592-9700

When to Visit: Wednesdays–Fridays—10 A.M. to 5 P.M. Saturdays and Sundays—noon to 5 P.M. Tuesdays—open to groups by appointment only

Charges/Fees: Suggested donations: adults—$3; seniors, children—$1.50

Suggested Grades: 1–adult

Guided Tour: Yes; 1–1½ hours

Maximum Group: 35

Group Notice: 1 month

Eating Facilities: None

Restroom Facilities: Yes

Handicapped Access: Yes

Gift Shop: Yes

Library/Research Facilities: Yes

By Subway: No. 7 to Willets Point–Shea Stadium

By Bus: Q48, Q58 or Q88

119 · QUEENS WILDLIFE CENTER

The 11-acre Queens Wildlife Center opened in June 1992 in Flushing Meadows–Corona Park, site of the 1939 and 1964 World's Fairs. This zoo, devoted primarily to North American animals, is divided into "wild" and "domestic" areas, featuring some 250 animals of 40 species. The wild side of the zoo leads visitors into pockets of North American wild habitats, from the Great Plains to the rocky California coast, to a Northeastern forest. It is home to mountain lions, bison, bobcats, coyotes, elk, sea lions and more. The center is also home to endangered spectacled bears from South America. They are part of the Species Survival Plan which, in cooperation with other zoos around the world, is designed to save species from extinction. The marsh exhibit area is an actual marsh habitat, a natural home for native wildlife. The area is a prime bird-watching site, with aquatic plants and birds. A geodesic-dome aviary—used in the 1964 World's Fair and updated for the center—features a winding walkway that leads visitors from the forest floor to the treetops at its apex. The center's domestic exhibits allow young visitors to view and touch animals such as sheep, rabbits and goats. It is also an education center where people of all ages can learn about wildlife and their habitats.

Address/Telephone: 53-51 111 Street, Queens, NY, (718) 271-7761

When to Visit: April–October: Mondays–Fridays—10 A.M. to 5 P.M. Saturdays, Sundays and holidays—10 A.M. to 5:30 P.M. November–March: Daily—10 A.M. to 4:30 P.M.

Charges/Fees: Adults—$2.50; seniors—$1.25; children (3–12)—$.50; children under 3—free

Suggested Grades: All grades

Guided Tour: Informal tours offered daily, once a day; 1 hour

Maximum Group: No maximum

Group Notice: None required

Eating Facilities: Yes

Restroom Facilities: Yes

Handicapped Access: Yes

Gift Shop: Yes

Library/Research Facilities: None

By Subway: No. 7 to 111 Street (walk south on 111 Street to Corona Park)

By Bus: Q23 or Q58

120 • SOCRATES SCULPTURE PARK

Founded in the mid-1980s, Socrates Sculpture Park was formerly a rubble-filled vacant lot. Sculptor Mark di Suvero conceived the idea of an outdoor, interactive studio and exhibition space in which artists can work and exhibit their projects and the public can often watch large-scale works in progress. The park mounts one or two exhibitions a year. The exhibits are hands-on shows, inviting audience participation.

Address/Telephone: Broadway at Vernon Boulevard, Queens, NY 11106, (718) 956-1819

Mailing Address: P.O. Box 6259, Queens, NY 11106

When to Visit: Every day—10 A.M. to sunset

Charges/Fees: Free

Suggested Grades: All grades

Guided Tour: Yes (tours vary according to group's needs)

Maximum Group: 50

Group Notice: 1 month preferred

Eating Facilities: None

Restroom Facilities: None

Handicapped Access: Yes

Gift Shop: None

Library/Research Facilities: None

By Subway: N to Broadway in Astoria, Queens

By Bus: Q103

STATEN ISLAND

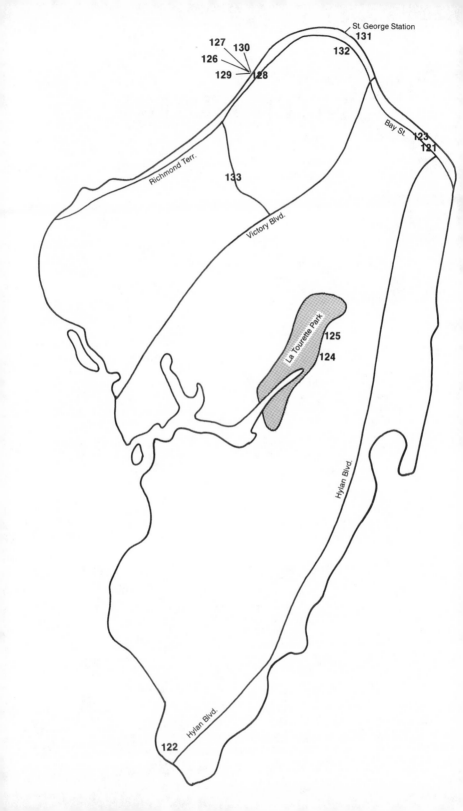

Alice Austen House. *(Photograph by V. Amesse)*

121 · ALICE AUSTEN HOUSE

"Clear Comfort," the home of Alice Austen (1866–1952) for nearly 80 years, has been restored to its appearance in the 1890s with the help of the famous photographer's extensive photographic records of the house and grounds, which command a superb view of the bay. Austen was one of the finest photographers of the nineteenth century, creating images on approximately 8000 glass plates, of which more than 3000 survive. Today changing exhibitions at the house museum explore themes inspired by the photographer's works and times, often using her own images.

Address/Telephone: 2 Hylan Boulevard (at Edgewater Street), Staten Island, NY 10305, (718) 816-4506

When to Visit: Thursdays–Sundays—noon to 5 P.M.

Days/Holidays Closed: Mondays–Wednesdays and all major holidays

Charges/Fees: Suggested donation—$2

Suggested Grades: 1–8

Guided Tour: Yes; 1 hour

Maximum Group: 54

Group Notice: 2-week minimum

Eating Facilities: None

Restroom Facilities: Yes

Handicapped Access: Yes

Gift Shop: Yes

Library/Research Facilities: Yes

Travel Directions: By subway from Manhattan, take the Nos. 1 or 9 to South Ferry, the N or R to Whitehall or Nos. 4 or 5 to Bowling Green. Take the Staten Island Ferry at Battery Park to the St. George terminal on Staten Island. Board the S51 bus to Hylan Boulevard and Bay Street, then walk east one block to house. By bus from Manhattan, take the M1, M6 or M15 to South Ferry, then follow directions above

122 · CONFERENCE HOUSE

On September 11, 1776, the last peace conference between delegates of the Continental Congress and the British government, hosted by Admiral Lord Howe, was held on Staten Island. John Adams, Edward Rutledge and Benjamin Franklin traveled from Philadelphia to Staten Island to hold one last conference in an attempt to prevent war. The meeting took place in the Billopp Manor House, built ca. 1680 by Captain Christopher Billopp, a Royal Navy officer who came to America in 1674. His descendants lived in the house until the American Revolution, at which time the State of New York confiscated the property of all pro-British colonists. For the next 150 years, the house passed from private owner to private owner, until 1925, when efforts to restore it began. In 1929 the house was placed under the care of the Conference House Association, which has restored the national landmark to its appearance during the famous peace conference. Today visitors can tour the house and grounds for a glimpse of Staten Island's Colonial history, including various demonstrations of daily activities. Special tours for school groups allow children to watch and participate in such activities as candle making, cooking and "touch-and-smell" tours of the rose and herb gardens.

Address/Telephone: 7455 Hylan Boulevard (off Satterlee Street), Staten Island, NY 10307, (718) 984-6046

Mailing Address: P.O. Box 171, Staten Island, NY 10307

When to Visit: Wednesdays–Sundays—1 P.M. to 4 P.M.

Days/Holidays Closed: December 15–March 15, Mondays, Tuesdays, Easter and Thanksgiving

Charges/Fees: Adults—$2; seniors, children under 12—$1

Suggested Grades: K–6

Guided Tour: Yes; approximately 30 minutes

Maximum Group: 20–25

Group Notice: 1 month

Eating Facilities: None. Picnic facilities available

Restroom Facilities: Yes (portables)

Handicapped Access: None

Gift Shop: Souvenirs
Library/Research Facilities: None
Travel Directions: By subway from Manhattan, take the Nos. 1 or 9 to South Ferry, the N or R to Whitehall Street or the Nos. 4 or 5 to Bowling Green. Take the Staten Island Ferry at Battery Park to the St. George terminal on Staten Island. Board the S78 bus to Craig Avenue

123 · GARIBALDI-MEUCCI MUSEUM

The Garibaldi-Meucci house is preserved as a memorial to the lives of Antonio Meucci and Giuseppe Garibaldi. In 1849 Meucci discovered that sound could be transmitted by electric wires; Alexander Graham Bell was then only two years old. Meucci's invention and life's work would have passed unnoticed except that he also extended refuge and sanctuary to Giuseppe Garibaldi, who had been forced to flee his homeland while fighting for the unification of Italy. Garibaldi lived in Meucci's home from 1850 to 1854. The museum preserves the culture and tradition of the Italian-American community through various programs and a video presentation with a curatorial guided tour. An Italian Culture for Children program (October–May) includes storytelling with music and costumes, history and an art workshop. Other offerings include free annual outdoor concerts, an art-and-architecture lecture series, adult Italian language classes and Italian needlework classes.

Address/Telephone: 420 Tompkins Avenue (at Chestnut Avenue), Staten Island, NY 10305, (718) 442-1608
When to Visit: Tuesdays–Sundays—1 P.M. to 5 P.M.
Days/Holidays Closed: Mondays, New Year's Day, Good Friday, Easter, July 4, Election Day, Thanksgiving and Christmas
Charges/Fees: Donations accepted
Suggested Grades: School programs available by appointment (October–June)
Guided Tour: Group tours by appointment only; 1–1½ hours. Individual tours daily
Maximum Group: 50
Group Notice: 4 weeks
Eating Facilities: None

Restroom Facilities: Yes
Handicapped Access: Yes
Gift Shop: None
Library/Research Facilities: Over 1200 volumes on Italian culture and history
Travel Directions: By subway from Manhattan, take Nos. 1 or 9 to South Ferry, the N or R to Whitehall Street or the Nos. 4 or 5 to Bowling Green. Take the Staten Island Ferry at Battery Park to the St. George terminal on Staten Island. Board the S52, S78 or S79 bus, all of which stop in front of the museum. By bus from Manhattan, take the M1, M6 or M15 to South Ferry, then follow directions above

124 · HISTORIC RICHMOND TOWN

Formally established in 1958, Historic Richmond Town is a historic village and museum complex interpreting three centuries of daily life and culture on Staten Island. Located on a 100-acre site, it includes a 30-acre exhibition center containing the original village center and 27 historic buildings dating from the seventeenth to the twentieth centuries. Many of the buildings have been relocated from other sites, restored and furnished with period pieces. In addition to tours of the village buildings there are historic exhibitions and demonstrations of daily activities of early Staten Islanders.

Address/Telephone: 441 Clarke Avenue, Staten Island, NY 10306, (718) 351-1611

When to Visit: Wednesdays–Sundays—1 P.M. to 5 P.M. (Extended hours during July and August)

Days/Holidays Closed: Mondays, Tuesdays, New Year's Day, Thanksgiving and Christmas

Charges/Fees: Adults—$4; seniors, students, children (6–18)—$2.50. Some special events have higher fees

Suggested Grades: All grades

Guided Tour: Guided tours available April–June, September–December; 1-1½ hours

Maximum Group: 60

Group Notice: 2 weeks for adult groups

Eating Facilities: Yes (snack bar). Picnic facilities available

Restroom Facilities: Yes

Handicapped Access: Limited

Gift Shop: Yes

Library/Research Facilities: By appointment only (very limited facilities)

Travel Directions: By subway from Manhattan, take Nos. 1 or 9 to South Ferry, the N or R to Whitehall or the Nos. 4 or 5 to Bowling Green. Take the Staten Island Ferry to the St. George terminal on Staten Island. Board the S74 bus to Richmond Town

125 • JACQUES MARCHAIS MUSEUM OF TIBETAN ART

Also known as the Tibetan Museum, the museum was founded in 1945 by Jacques Marchais (the professional name of Mrs. Jacqueline Klauber). Designed to resemble a small Tibetan mountain temple, the museum houses a collection of Tibetan, Tibeto-Chinese, Nepalese and Mongolian pieces from the seventeenth to nineteenth centuries. The collection is rich in metal figures of deities and lamas as well as in paintings; there are also examples of jewel-encrusted Nepalese metalwork, a set of silver ceremonial implements used by a previous Panchen Lama, jewelry, dance masks and imperial Chinese cloisonné decorative objects. The museum offers a variety of community and school programs to promote understanding of Tibetan art and culture.

Address/Telephone: 338 Lighthouse Avenue (near Richmond Road), Staten Island, NY 10306, (718) 987-3478 (recorded information); (718) 987-3500 (staff/office)

Mailing Address: P.O. Box 060198, Staten Island, NY 10306-1217

When to Visit: April–November: Wednesdays–Sundays—1 P.M. to 5 P.M. December–March: By appointment only

Days/Holidays Closed: Mondays and Tuesdays (April–November)

Charges/Fees: Adults—$3; seniors—$2.50; children—$1

Suggested Grades: 1–adult

Guided Tour: Yes; 1-1½ hours

Maximum Group: Children, 35; adults, 45

Group Notice: 3-4 weeks

Eating Facilities: None. Picnic facilities available in the gardens
Restroom Facilities: Yes
Handicapped Access: None
Gift Shop: Yes
Library/Research Facilities: By appointment only
Travel Directions: By subway from Manhattan, take Nos. 1 or 9 to South Ferry, the N or R to Whitehall Street or Nos. 4 or 5 to Bowling Green. Take the Staten Island Ferry at Battery Park to the St. George terminal on Staten Island. Board the S74 bus to Lighthouse Avenue and Richmond Road. Turn right and walk up the hill to the museum entrance. By bus from Manhattan, take the M1, M6 or M15 to South Ferry, then follow directions above

126 · JOHN A. NOBLE COLLECTION AT SNUG HARBOR CULTURAL CENTER

Staten Island's newest museum, the John A. Noble Collection is devoted to the works and life of the nationally noted maritime artist (1913–1983). The collection includes Noble's series of 79 lithographs depicting twentieth-century maritime endeavor, his paintings, 600 of his "rowboat sketches," various maritime memorabilia and a collection of 5000 photographs of New York Harbor.

Address/Telephone: Snug Harbor Cultural Center, 1000 Richmond Terrace, Staten Island, NY 10301, (718) 447-6490
When to Visit: Mondays–Fridays—9 A.M. to 2 P.M.
Days/Holidays Closed: Saturdays, Sundays and all major holidays
Charges/Fees: Free
Suggested Grades: All grades
Guided Tour: None
Maximum Group: 25–30
Group Notice: 2 weeks–1 month
Eating Facilities: Yes (Melville's Café at Snug Harbor Cultural Center). Picnic facilities available
Restroom Facilities: Yes
Handicapped Access: None
Gift Shop: Yes
Library/Research Facilities: Yes
Travel Directions: By subway from Manhattan, take Nos. 1 or 9 to South Ferry, the N or R to Whitehall Street or the Nos. 4 or 5 to Bowling Green. Take the Staten Island Ferry at Battery Park to the St. George terminal on Staten Island. Board the S40 bus, which stops across the street from the Snug Harbor Cultural Center on Richmond Terrace. By bus from Manhattan, take the M1, M6 or M15 to South Ferry, then follow directions above

127 · NEWHOUSE CENTER FOR CONTEMPORARY ART AT SNUG HARBOR CULTURAL CENTER

The Newhouse Center features exhibitions of emerging and mid-career artists working in all media, contemporary craft art and interdisciplinary programs that embrace diverse cultures and art forms. The nationally acclaimed outdoor Sculpture Festival runs every year from June through October.

Address/Telephone: Snug Harbor Cultural Center, 1000 Richmond Terrace, Staten Island, NY 10301, (718) 448-2500

When to Visit: Wednesdays–Sundays—noon to 5 P.M.

Days/Holidays Closed: Mondays, Tuesdays, New Year's Day, Thanksgiving and Christmas

Charges/Fees: Suggested donation—$2

Guided Tour: The Newhouse Center is included in the free tour of Snug Harbor Cultural Center offered Saturdays and Sundays at 2 P.M. For tours of the Newhouse Center Gallery, call Group Tours at (718) 448-2500

Group Notice: Call Group Tours for reservation information

Eating Facilities: Yes (Melville's Café at Snug Harbor Cultural Center open: Tuesdays–Fridays—11 A.M. to 2 P.M. Saturdays and Sundays—noon to 5 P.M.)

Restroom Facilities: Yes

Handicapped Access: Yes

Travel Directions: By subway from Manhattan, take Nos. 1 or 9 to South Ferry, the N or R to Whitehall Street or Nos. 4 or 5 to Bowling Green. Take the Staten Island Ferry at Battery Park to the St. George terminal on Staten Island. Board the S40 bus, which stops across the street from the center on Richmond Terrace. By bus from Manhattan, take the M1, M6 or M15 to South Ferry, then follow directions above

128 · SNUG HARBOR CULTURAL CENTER

Snug Harbor Cultural Center is located on 83 acres of parkland and consists of 28 historic buildings. A collection of nineteenth-century Greek Revival, Beaux-Arts, Second Empire and Italianate architecture, it is being preserved and adapted for the visual and performing arts. The center was originally founded in 1801 as a maritime hospital and home for retired sailors—the first in the United States. Snug Harbor was purchased by the City of New York in the early 1970s and opened as a cultural center in 1976. Today the center provides concerts year-round, contemporary-art exhibitions and education programs—all in a unique setting, rich with maritime history and surrounded by beautiful grounds. The center is also home to the Newhouse Center for Contemporary Arts, the Staten Island Children's Museum, the Staten Island Botanical Garden and the John A. Noble Collection (see individual entries).

Address/Telephone: 1000 Richmond Terrace (at Snug Harbor Road), Staten Island, NY 10301, (718) 448-2500

When to Visit: Grounds are open daily from dawn to dusk. Open evenings for classes and concerts

Days/Holidays Closed: New Year's Day, Thanksgiving and Christmas

Charges/Fees: Admission to the grounds—free

Suggested Grades: All grades

Guided Tour: Guided tours for individuals on Saturdays and Sundays, 2 P.M.—free. Group

tours by appointment—$5 per person. Call the Snug Harbor Education Department for more information (718) 448-2500

Maximum Group: 50

Group Notice: 2-week minimum

Eating Facilities: Yes (Melville's Café). Picnic facilities available; catered lunches by appointment

Restroom Facilities: Yes

Handicapped Access: Yes

Gift Shop: Yes (Wednesdays–Sundays, 1 P.M. to 4:30 P.M.)

Library/Research Facilities: None

Travel Directions: By subway from Manhattan, take Nos. 1 or 9 to South Ferry, the N or R to Whitehall Street or Nos. 4 or 5 to Bowling Green. Take the Staten Island Ferry at Battery Park to the St. George terminal on Staten Island. Board the S40 bus, which stops across the street from the center on Richmond Terrace

129 · STATEN ISLAND BOTANICAL GARDEN AT SNUG HARBOR CULTURAL CENTER

Established in 1975, the Staten Island Botanical Garden includes an English Perennial Garden, a White Garden (featuring blooms in white and gray), a Butterfly Garden with plants particularly attractive to butterflies, a Rose Garden set on more than one-third of an acre and a permanent display of tropical plants and orchids, specimen trees and shrubs in the conservatory. The Lions Sensory Garden is designed to specially serve the physically challenged; accessible pathways and raised planting beds allow visitors in wheelchairs to smell and touch the plantings.

Address/Telephone: Snug Harbor Cultural Center, 1000 Richmond Terrace, Staten Island, NY 10301, (718) 273-8200

When to Visit: Grounds—daylight hours. Conservatory—May through September: Mondays–Fridays—9 A.M. to 5 P.M. Saturdays and Sundays—noon to 4 P.M.

Days/Holidays Closed: Conservatory: closed October–April

Charges/Fees: Free

Guided Tour: By appointment only

Maximum Group: Call for details

Group Notice: Call for details

Eating Facilities: Yes (Melville's Café at Snug Harbor Cultural Center). Picnic facilities available

Restroom Facilities: Yes

Handicapped Access: Yes

Gift Shop: Yes

Library/Research Facilities: Open to members only

Travel Directions: By subway from Manhattan, take Nos. 1 or 9 to South Ferry, the N or R to Whitehall Street or the Nos. 4 or 5 to Bowling Green. Take the Staten Island Ferry at Battery Park to the St. George terminal on Staten Island. Board the S40 bus, which stops across the street from the Snug Harbor Cultural Center on Richmond Terrace. By bus from Manhattan, take the M1, M6 or M15 to South Ferry, then follow directions above

130 · STATEN ISLAND CHILDREN'S MUSEUM AT SNUG HARBOR CULTURAL CENTER

The Staten Island Children's Museum moved to its new, permanent home at Snug Harbor Cultural Center in 1986. The museum is a place where a child's natural curiosity, imagination and exuberance are tools for discovery. A private, nonprofit educational institution chartered by New York State in 1974, the museum creates and presents exhibits and programs based on themes in the arts, humanities and sciences. School and community programs are developed around an exhibit's theme and range from tours and art workshops to all-day family arts festivals on the grounds of Snug Harbor.

Address/Telephone: Snug Harbor Cultural Center, 1000 Richmond Terrace (at Snug Harbor Road), Staten Island, NY 10301, (718) 273-2060

When to Visit: School-year hours: Tuesdays–Sundays—noon to 5 P.M. Summer hours: Tuesdays–Sundays—11 A.M. to 5 P.M.

Days/Holidays Closed: Closed for 2 weeks every September, Mondays, Memorial Day, Easter, July 4, Labor Day and Christmas

Charges/Fees: General—$3.25; children under 2—free

Suggested Grades: Pre-K to 7

Guided Tour: Call for details

Maximum Group: Call for details

Group Notice: Call for details

Eating Facilities: Yes (Melville's Café; vending machines in museum building). Picnic facilities available

Restroom Facilities: Yes

Handicapped Access: Yes

Gift Shop: Yes

Library/Research Facilities: None

Travel Directions: By subway from Manhattan, take Nos. 1 or 9 to South Ferry, the N or R to Whitehall Street or Nos. 4 or 5 to Bowling Green. Take the Staten Island Ferry at Battery Park to the St. George terminal on Staten Island. Board the S40 bus, which stops across the street from the center on Richmond Terrace. By bus from Manhattan, take the M1, M6 or M15 to South Ferry, then follow directions above

131 · STATEN ISLAND FERRY AND THE STATEN ISLAND FERRY COLLECTION

Touted as the best bargain in New York City ($.50 a round-trip), the five-mile ride aboard the Staten Island Ferry offers the only complete view of New York Harbor, including the Brooklyn Bridge, Manhattan skyline, the Statue of Liberty and Ellis Island, Robin's Reef Lighthouse and the Verrazano-Narrows Bridge. In the waiting room of the St. George terminal on Staten Island, the Ferry Collection exhibition (presented by the Staten Island Institute of Arts and Sciences) celebrates the history of the ferry line (founded in 1810 by Cornelius Vanderbilt) in striking displays of artifacts, historic postcards, photographs and scale models of vintage ferries. Special guided Staten Island Ferry rides are available to groups and can be combined with the institute's other group programs. Special classes are also available to school groups.

Address/Telephone: Staten Island Ferry, South Ferry Terminal (at Whitehall Street), New York, NY 10004, (212) 806-6940; Staten Island Ferry Collection of SIIAS, Staten Island Ferry Terminal, St. George, Staten Island, NY 10301, (718) 727-1135

Mailing Address: Staten Island Ferry, Department of Ferries, Room 301, Battery Maritime Building, New York, NY 10004; Staten Island Ferry Collection of SIIAS, c/o Staten Island Institute of Arts and Sciences, 75 Stuyvesant Place, Staten Island, NY 10301-1998

When to Visit: Staten Island Ferry: daily—24 hours a day. The Ferry Collection: daily—9 A.M. to 2 P.M.

Days/Holidays Closed: The Ferry Collection: closed major holidays

Charges/Fees: Staten Island Ferry (round-trip fares): general—$.50; seniors—$.25. The Ferry Collection (suggested donations): adults—$1; children 12 and under—$.25

Suggested Grades: All grades

Guided Tour: Guided Staten Island Ferry rides include museum tour; 1–1½ hours. Call (718) 727-1135 for information

Maximum Group: Group prices and tours based on 15-person minimum

Group Notice: 4-week minimum

Eating Facilities: Yes (see Staten Island Institute of Arts and Sciences entry for details)

Restroom Facilities: Yes

Handicapped Access: Yes

Gift Shop: The maritime museum store at Staten Island Ferry Collection

Library/Research Facilities: None

Travel Directions: By subway from Manhattan, take Nos. 1 or 9 to South Ferry, the N or R to Whitehall Street or Nos. 4 or 5 to Bowling Green. Take the Staten Island Ferry at Battery Park to the St. George terminal on Staten Island. By bus from Manhattan, take the M1, M6 or M15 to South Ferry, then follow directions above

Additional Information: For Staten Island Ferry information call (212) 806-6940

132 · STATEN ISLAND INSTITUTE OF ARTS AND SCIENCES

Drawing on a collection of more than two million items, this museum, founded in 1881, displays objects related to local history, contemporary and regional art, regional natural history, decorative arts, family history, antiques and more. "The Staten Island Biennial Juried Art Exhibition" is the borough's premier showcase for regional and national contemporary art, running from September to January of even-numbered years. "The Staten Island Biennial Juried Craft Exhibition" is held during odd-numbered years. The institute also offers activities for all age groups, educational programs, group gallery tours, walking tours, guided Staten Island Ferry rides and more. An extensive archives and library is available to researchers, as are the institute's natural-history collections.

Address/Telephone: 75 Stuyvesant Place (at Wall Street), Staten Island, NY 10301-1998, (718) 727-1135

When to Visit: Mondays–Saturdays—9 A.M. to 5 P.M. Sundays—1 P.M. to 5 P.M.

Days/Holidays Closed: Major holidays

Charges/Fees: Suggested donations: general— $2.50; seniors, students—$1.50

Suggested Grades: All grades (programs available for ages 3 to adult)

Guided Tour: Various group tour options; 1 hour

Maximum Group: Cost for groups are based

on a 15-person minimum; no maximum group size (large groups will be broken up)

Group Notice: 4-week minimum

Eating Facilities: For groups, a choice of catered buffet luncheons or boxed lunches is offered. Picnic facilities available

Restroom Facilities: Yes

Handicapped Access: Limited

Gift Shop: Yes

Library/Research Facilities: Yes

Travel Directions: By subway from Manhattan, take the Nos. 1 or 9 to South Ferry, the N or R to Whitehall Street or the Nos. 4 or 5 to

Bowling Green. Take the Staten Island Ferry to the St. George terminal on Staten Island. The institute is 2 blocks away from the ferry terminal. By bus from Manhattan, take the

M1, M6 or M15 to South Ferry, then follow directions above

Additional Information: Call for travel directions by car

133 · STATEN ISLAND ZOO

New York's "Biggest Little Zoo" includes a wraparound aquarium with local and exotic fish including sharks and moray eels. The Serpentarium houses a world-renowned reptile and North American rattlesnake collection, and there is a representation of an endangered South American tropical forest. The Children's Zoo, in a New England farm setting, offers hands-on activities for children. There are also indoor and outdoor mammal and bird exhibits—all on an eight-acre, beautifully landscaped park. The zoo sponsors year-round adult and children's educational programs and local, national and international travel programs.

Address/Telephone: 614 Broadway, Staten Island, NY 10310, (718) 442-3100
When to Visit: Daily—10 A.M. to 4:45 P.M.
Days/Holidays Closed: New Year's Day, Thanksgiving and Christmas
Charges/Fees: Adults—$3; children (3–11)—$2; members and children under 3—free. Wednesdays, 2 P.M. to 4:45 P.M.—free
Suggested Grades: All grades
Guided Tour: None
Eating Facilities: Yes (snack bar)
Restroom Facilities: Yes
Travel Directions: By subway from Manhattan,

take Nos. 1 or 9 to South Ferry, the N or R to Whitehall Street or Nos. 4 or 5 to Bowling Green. Take the Staten Island Ferry to the St. George terminal on Staten Island. Board the S48 bus to Forest Avenue and Broadway. Turn left on Broadway and walk 2½ blocks to the zoo entrance. By bus from Manhattan, take the M1, M6 or M15 to South Ferry, then follow directions above. From Brooklyn, take the S53 bus, which originates in Bay Ridge at 95 Street and Fourth Avenue (near the BMT subway), to the Broadway entrance to the zoo

· TIBETAN MUSEUM: see JACQUES MARCHAIS MUSEUM OF TIBETAN ART

INDEX